CULTURE SMART!
TURKEY

Charlotte McPherson

·K·U·P·E·R·A·R·D·

ISBN 978 1 85733 693 1
This book is also available as an e-book: eISBN 978 1 85733 694 8

British Library Cataloguing in Publication Data
A CIP catalogue entry for this book is available from the British Library

First published in Great Britain
by Kuperard, an imprint of Bravo Ltd
59 Hutton Grove, London N12 8DS
Tel: +44 (0) 20 8446 2440   Fax: +44 (0) 20 8446 2441
www.culturesmart.co.uk
Inquiries: sales@kuperard.co.uk

Distributed in the United States and Canada
by Random House Distribution Services
1745 Broadway, New York, NY 10019
Tel: +1 (212) 572-2844   Fax: +1 (212) 572-4961
Inquiries: csorders@randomhouse.com

Series Editor Geoffrey Chesler
Design Bobby Birchall

Printed in Malaysia

About the Author

CHARLOTTE McPHERSON is an American who has lived in Turkey since 1979. For her graduate studies at Indiana University she specialized in Uralic Altaic languages and history. She has an MA in Anthropology, and during the 1980s she conducted extensive research in Turkey and Central Asia among Turkic-speaking peoples. She has lectured in Social Anthropology at Mimar Sinan University, Istanbul, and has written many scholarly papers and several books. She is currently Vice President of the Turkish-American Cultural Association in Istanbul, where she owns and manages a major English-language bookstore, Greenhouse.

**The Culture Smart! series is continuing to expand.
For further information and latest titles visit
www.culturesmart.co.uk**

The publishers would like to thank **CultureSmart!**Consulting for its help in researching and developing the concept for this series.

CultureSmart!Consulting creates tailor-made seminars and consultancy programs to meet a wide range of corporate, public-sector, and individual needs. Whether delivering courses on multicultural team building in the USA, preparing Chinese engineers for a posting in Europe, training call-center staff in India, or raising the awareness of police forces to the needs of diverse ethnic communities, it provides essential, practical, and powerful skills worldwide to an increasingly international workforce.

For details, visit www.culturesmartconsulting.com

CultureSmart!Consulting and **CultureSmart!** guides have both contributed to and featured regularly in the weekly travel program "Fast Track" on BBC World TV.

contents

contents

Map of Turkey

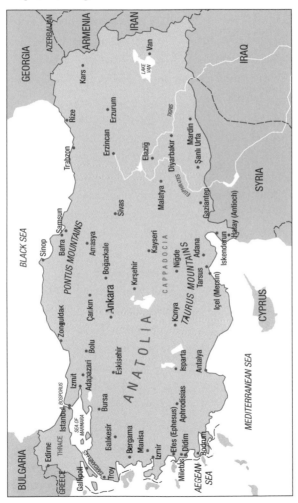

introduction

Turkey has always attracted travelers. Over the centuries the landmass of Asia Minor, heart of the great multicultural Ottoman Empire and now the modern Republic of Turkey, experienced waves of migrations in which one civilization displaced another, leaving a unique and glorious cultural heritage. Its heroic landscapes, magnificent ruins, miles of stunning beaches, and legendary hospitality continue to draw visitors to its shores.

At first glance, Turkey seems Westernized and modern in many ways—but this appearance is misleading. It is a land of contrasts, a heady mixture of Oriental mystery and romance and ultramodern city life, deep-rooted religious faith and determined secularism, a fierce sense of national pride and openness to foreign ideas. Turkish culture is a distinctive blend of European and Middle Eastern ways of life.

One remarkable man was responsible for creating modern Turkey. In 1923 Mustafa Kemal (known as Atatürk, "the Father of the Turks") took control and transformed the country from an absolute feudal monarchy to today's secular, democratic Muslim state. Tales of this one-man revolution abound, and he is genuinely universally revered. His image is still everywhere, and his legacy a source of national pride. Patriotism is a Turkish virtue, and the army is regarded as the defender of Atatürk's secular democracy. Even Turkey's Islamic movement is committed to the separation of religion and state.

The Turkish people are very much their own center of gravity, and for the unwary visitor there are pitfalls to avoid as well as great riches to be found. *Culture Smart! Turkey* aims to help you understand the paradoxes of Turkish life. It outlines the complex history of Anatolia, and particularly the formative years after the First World War. It provides key insights into Turkish values and attitudes, describes important customs and traditions, and reveals what life is like for the Turks at home, at work, and at play. It offers practical tips and information about what to expect and how to behave in different situations.

This fascinating and important country is not only the cradle of European and Islamic cultures: it offers opportunities for business development, academic studies, and enjoyable exploration. The Turks are very hospitable, open, and pleased to meet foreigners. If you show an interest in their culture and respect for their point of view they will repay your effort many times over.

Key Facts

Official Name	Turkiye Cumhuriyeti (Republic of Turkey)	Turkey is a member of NATO, the Council of Europe, and an associate member of the European Union.
Capital City	Ankara	Population approx. 5 million
Main Cities	Istanbul. Officiallly the population is 14 million; unofficially between 16 and 18 million.	Other cities: Izmir, Bursa, Adana, Gaziantep, Konya, Antalya, Diyarbakır, Mersin
Population	75.6 million approx.	
Area	301,382 sq. miles (780,580 sq. km.) 97% in Asia and 3% in Europe.	
Climate	Varies considerably. The Black Sea coast is mild with a lot of rain. Middle and eastern Anatolia have hot, dry summers and cold winters. A typical Mediterranean climate is common along the Aegean and Mediterranean Seas.	
Language	Turkish, written in the Latin script	Minority languages incl. Kurdish, Arabic, Armenian, Greek
Religion	Turkey is a secular republic: 99.8% of people are Muslim.	Other religions: Christianity and Judaism.

Government	Secular democratic republic	Executive Power resides in the Grand National Assembly, which elects the President of the state for a period of seven years. The President appoints the Prime Minister as head of government.
Currency	Turkish Lira (TRY)	1 TRY = 0.51 USD 1 USD = 1.98 TRY (2013)
Media	TRT is the national TV and radio network. There are numerous local and commercial satellite stations.	There are numerous private radio stations. Various newspapers and magazines in Turkish, English, and other languages are available.
Electricity	220 volts (50 Hz)	2-pronged plugs used
DVD/Video	TV/Video is Pal system; some systems will pay NTSC.	DVD is European region; video players have largely been replaced by DVD players.
Internet Domain	.tr	
Telephone	Turkey's country code is 90.	To dial out of Turkey, dial 00 and then the country code.
Time Zone	GMT + 2 hours	

LAND &
PEOPLE

GEOGRAPHICAL SNAPSHOT

Situated at the southeastern corner of Europe,
Turkey straddles the straits that divide Europe and
Asia—the Dardanelles, the Sea of Marmara, and
the Bosporus. Three percent of its landmass lies in
Europe, giving it borders with Greece and Bulgaria,
while 97 percent lies in Asia. The enormous Asian
part, known as Anatolia, shares borders on the east
and south with Georgia, Armenia, Azerbaijan, Iran,
Iraq, and Syria. The country is bounded on three
sides by water: the Aegean Sea to the west, the
Mediterranean to the south, and the Black Sea to
the north.

European Turkey is the most densely populated
part of the country. In Anatolia, the population
is densest in the west, in urban centers such as
Istanbul, Bursa, Izmir, and Izmit, and decreases
steadily toward the east. In the interior the
population is concentrated along the paths of rivers
and in towns such as Ankara, Eskişehir, Konya,
Erzurum, Malatya, and Kayseri. Most of the Central
Anatolian Highlands consist of undulating hills
and broad, high plateaus from which mountains
occasionally rise. The population of the south coast
is massed on the fertile plains of Antalya and Adana,

as well as in the province of Hatay, with its port of Iskenderun. There is a steady trend of people moving into the cities from rural areas However, in the past decade the Turkish government, in order to prevent further migration to urban centers has been working hard to mix historic preservation and urban revitalization with community development and sustainable tourism in eastern Turkey.

Enclosing the Central Anatolian Highlands are two great mountain ranges: the Pontus Mountains in the north, and the Taurus range to the south. The most famous mountain is Mount Ararat in the east, where Noah's ark is reputed to have come to rest. Turkey is rich in water, the lifeblood of the Middle East. The most important rivers of the region, the Tigris and the Euphrates, each have their source here.

CLIMATE
Turkey's latitude would lead one to expect a broadly temperate or Mediterranean climate. Owing to its topography, however, the country's climate varies

according to region. Turks claim that all four seasons can be experienced in any one day, albeit in different parts of the country.

The Black Sea coast has a predominantly mild summer and winter. It is the area with the heaviest rainfall (pack an umbrella for a trip here!) and is famous for its tea plantations.

The Mediterranean and Aegean coasts have a typical Mediterranean climate, with long, hot, dry summers and mild winters.

The Marmara coast is a climatic transitional zone between the first two. It is hot, but does not have such dry summers. The winters are cool, with occasional frosts and outbreaks of snow.

Central Anatolia has a markedly continental climate, with hot summers around 86°F (30°C), and bitterly cold, snowy winters, sometimes down to -22°F (-30°C). There are large temperature swings between day and night and even in summer the nights can be surprisingly cool.

A BRIEF HISTORY
When the Turks entered Anatolia in the eleventh century they encountered a cosmopolitan civilization that was itself the product of many earlier traditions. Turkish tolerance, pluralism, and openness to new ideas led to a cultural exchange that resulted in an extraordinary flowering of Islamic humanism. They created a great inclusive empire that transformed the societies they absorbed and lasted nearly a thousand years. Turks are proud not only of their own remarkable achievements, but of

the fact that the ancient civilizations of their homeland are part of the inheritance of mankind.

Early Anatolian Civilizations
Sophisticated Neolithic (8000–5000 BCE) settlements with religious shrines, decorated houses, and pottery dating to the seventh and sixth millennia BCE, have been found at Hacilar and Çatalhöyük in central Anatolia.

In the Bronze Age (3000–2000 BCE) two remarkable civilizations arose: the Mesopotamian-influenced Hatti in central and southeastern Anatolia, and the Mycenean settlement of Troy in northwestern Anatolia.

At the beginning of the second millennium BCE, an Indo-European people, the Hittites, entered Anatolia via the Caucasus and gradually absorbed the Hatti. Their powerful empire, with its capital at Hattusas (Boghazkoi), vied with Egypt for domination of the Near East in the thirteenth century BCE.

Roughly contemporary with the Hittites were the Mitani, who spoke Hurrian, in eastern Anatolia, and the civilization of Troy VI, the great walled Ilion of Homer's *Iliad* that commanded the Hellespont (the Dardanelles).

Around 1200 BCE, invasions by Indo-European tribes from Thrace utterly destroyed Troy and Hattusas, and a dark age followed. By the Iron Age (c. 1000 BCE) Anatolia was divided into numerous principalities of different size, ethnicity, and culture.

They included the Late Hittites in southeastern Anatolia and north Syria, the Urartians in the region of Lake Van and parts of Iran, the Phrygians in central and southeastern Anatolia, the Lydians, Carians, and Lycians in the west and southwest, and, on the western coastal fringe, the Ionians.

One of these invading tribes, the Phrygians, became a major power and established its capital at Gordion, between Ankara and Eskişehir. The last Phrygian king, Midas (c. 715 BCE), was recognized by the court of Sargon II of Assyria. His monuments still remain around Eskişehir.

The Lydian kingdom (750–300 BCE) was the first to invent a system of coinage, which revolutionized commerce. Sardis, the capital, was reputedly the richest city in the ancient world because of its gold mines. The wealth and might of its last king, Croesus, became proverbial.

Ionian Greeks began colonizing the western coast of Anatolia in around 1050 BCE. Their city-states included Miletus and Ephesus. In their most brilliant period, in the sixth century BCE, they gave the world philosophy and free scientific thought and became the center of poetry and the arts.

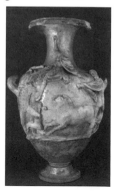

After the defeat of Croesus of Lydia by Cyrus the Great of Persia in 546 BCE, Anatolia came under Persian rule. For the first time in its history it served as a bridge between Asia and Europe—the Royal Road built by the Persians joined Iran to the Aegean coast.

The Hellenistic Age (333–30 BCE)
Alexander the Great's victory over the Persians at the Battle of Issus in 333 BCE restored the independence of Anatolia's Hellenistic cities, which regained their cultural supremacy. After Alexander's death the western Anatolian kingdom of Pergamum rivaled Alexandria in cultural, scientific, and artistic achievement.

The Roman Age (30 BCE–395 CE)
Through a combination of inheritance, conquest, and alliances, Rome began to establish provinces in Anatolia from the second century BCE. Pergamum became the western province of Asia. Other provinces were Bithynia and Pontus, Galatia, Pisidia, Cilicia, and Cappadocia. Julius Caesar reportedly uttered the words "I came, I saw, I conquered" when announcing his victory over Pharnaces of Pontus at Zela, near modern-day Tokat, in 47 BCE. Anatolia prospered within the Roman Empire. Luxurious new cities were built using the latest Roman design and technology. By the second century CE, Anatolia's cities rivaled Rome itself.

Byzantine Civilization (330–1453 CE)
In a real sense, Anatolia was the cradle of Christianity: Saint Paul was born in Tarsus in Cilicia. Many of his missionary journeys in the first century CE were to Anatolian cities—Ephesus, Konya, Troas, Miletus, Colossae. Followers of Christ were first called "Christians" in Antioch, near the

Syrian border. Many of Paul's epistles, and those of Peter, were written to believers in Anatolia. The Seven Churches of the Book of Revelation were all in western Anatolia. In 325 CE the first general council of the Church met in Nicea (Iznik), where it proclaimed the doctrine of the Trinity and established the Nicene Creed.

In 330 CE Constantine the Great made the ancient city of Byzantium the eastern capital of the Roman Empire and renamed it Constantinople. After the fall of Rome in the fifth century, the eastern Empire—which continued to consider itself Roman—presided over a civilization that lasted a thousand years, spanned the Middle Ages, and played a vital role in the interchange of ideas between East and West. Constantinople became one of the most important intellectual and cultural centers in the world.

The Arrival of the Turks
The ancestors of the modern Turks were nomadic tribesmen who lived on the steppes of Inner Asia in the sixth century CE. Over the next thousand years, after a series of conquests, different Turkic clans created a succession of multicultural, polyethnic empires that stretched from China to the Mediterranean. The Oghuz Turks moved west to Transoxiana (roughly, modern-day Uzbekistan and southwest Kazakhstan), where they settled and

embraced Islam, before migrating south to Iran.
There they founded the Great Seljuk State, which
created an inclusive Turkic, Arab, and Persian
culture. Waves of breakaway tribes from the Oghuz
confederation started entering Anatolia, where each
would establish a kingdom, only to fall to the next
Turkic group to come their way.

By 1000 CE the Byzantine Empire was fading
away. The seat of the Empire, Constantinople, was
on the European shore of the Bosporus. The last
successful Emperor, Basil II (976–1025 CE), was
succeeded by weak rulers who failed to maintain
the city's defenses.

In the eleventh century, the Caliph of Baghdad,
the supreme religious leader of Islam, recruited
Seljuk mercenaries to help him maintain his
position. As a result, their leader, Tughrul, was made
Sultan of Sunni Islam. The Seljuks assumed control
of Baghdad, and soon their empire covered most of
modern Turkey, Iraq, and Iran.

In 1071 CE the Byzantine army of Emperor
Romanus IV Diogenes was utterly defeated by the
Seljuk Turks at Manzikert, near Lake Van in the east.
Six years later the Seljuks founded a new state in
Rum, which is what the Muslims called the Eastern
Roman Empire.

The Seljuk Sultanate
Following a major defeat during the First Crusade
in 1097 CE, the Rum Seljuks set up their capital at
Konya, formerly Iconium, in central southern
Anatolia. This city stood at a crossroads and had
long served as a conduit for the ideas and influences

of nations of diverse ethnicity, language, and culture. There the Seljuks presided over a cultural renaissance, building magnificent mosques, academies, and centers of trade.

Ruins and ancient mosques testify to the splendor of Seljuk architecture. The period is famous for developing the use of brickwork, which enabled buildings to be decorated with reliefs. The Seljuks took full advantage of the strong sunlight in Turkey, Iran, and Iraq to create an elaborate interplay of light and shade, with the use of large portals, processional courtyards, vivid color, and intricate masonry. Their literature includes the mystical works of the great Sufi poets Rumi and Yunus Emre.

In the twelfth century CE the Byzantine Empire was shrinking, but the Seljuks were also in trouble, under pressure from Crusaders in the west and the Mongols in the east. In the 1190s invasions and civil war gradually brought the Seljuk Empire to near collapse, and in 1243 CE the Mongols defeated the Seljuks at Kösedagh. Seljuk power was completely broken by 1261.

The Rise of the Ottomans
As a result of the Mongol ascendancy in Iran, Asia Minor experienced a fresh influx of displaced Oghuz Turkic tribes in the thirteenth century. The Ottoman Turks, named after their leader Osman I

(1270–1326), emerged as a local power on the Byzantine-Seljuk frontier in northwestern Anatolia. In the late 1200s, Osman established the Janissaries as an elite fighting force to expand his kingdom. The Ottoman state spread rapidly, occupying the entire Asian side of the Sea of Marmara by 1304. In 1326, Bursa became its capital. In 1350, the Ottomans crossed the Dardenelles. The capital was moved to Edirne (old Adrianapolis) in Western Thrace in 1361, and from there the Ottomans began to penetrate the Balkans. Strategically positioned, practically encircling Constantinople, they slowly sapped the remaining power of the Byzantine emperors.

The clash of empires was also one of religion. Byzantium was the Holy Eastern Roman Empire. The Ottoman state was Muslim. To the political title of Sultan, the Ottoman rulers would add the spiritual title of Caliph (in 1517, when Mameluke Cairo was added to their lands). Despite this, during the course of the thirteenth and fourteenth centuries close economic and social ties had developed between Byzantium and Anatolia, particularly after the sack of Orthodox Constantinople by the Latin Crusaders in 1204.

Osman's grandson, Murad I, crushed a Christian coalition at Kosovo in 1389, gaining Serbia and the Balkans. The Byzantine Emperor was forced to acknowledge the Sultan as his overlord. Murad's successor, Beyazit I, defeated the last great crusade, led by Sigismund of Hungary, at Nicopolis in 1396. He then laid siege to Constantinople in 1397.

A new front opened up against the Ottomans in the east, however, when the Mongol threat resurfaced. Under the leadership of the Turco-Mongol conqueror Timur (Tamerlane), they defeated the Ottomans in a great battle on a plain near Ankara in 1402, capturing Beyazit and forcing him to raise the siege of Constantinople. This temporarily eased the pressure on the Byzantine Empire. However, the Tartars plundered Anatolia and moved on; their aim was to vanquish their enemies, not to expand to the west.

After internecine fighting among the sons of Beyazit, Murad II recovered the lost Ottoman lands and expanded their territory in southeastern Europe, paving the way for a fresh assault on Constantinople.

The Fall of Constantinople
Murad's successor, Mehmet II (1415–81), resolved to capture Constantinople for Islam. Although by now a weakened vassal state, Constantinople was home to Venetian and Genoese fleets that could cut the Turkish realm in two. In 1452, in just four months, Mehmet II built the fortress of Rumeli Hisar on the European side of the Bosporus north of Constantinople, thus closing the Bosporus to the city. The city walls were strong and fiercely defended, and access to the Golden Horn was barred by a great chain that stretched from shore to shore. Mehmet's masterstroke was to construct a huge causeway that enabled his army to haul their boats overland from the shore of the Bosporus into the Golden Horn, thus launching a naval attack from the north. The city walls were breached on May 29, 1453, and one glorious chapter in history came to a bloody end, to be succeeded by another.

This victory confirmed the Ottoman's European Empire. Mehmet II became known as Mehmet the Conqueror. He made Constantinople his capital, renamed it Istanbul, and settled it with people from different parts of his realm. In the years that followed he built palaces, markets, mosques, and religious  colleges. An intellectual steeped in Western classical culture—he spoke six languages, including Latin and Greek—Mehmet employed Greek and Italian advisers, and commissioned works by Italian artists.

The Ottoman Empire

The Empire attained its greatest glory in the reign of Süleyman the Magnificent (1520–66). This was a golden age in which magnificent palaces and mosques were built, including the Sülemaniye Mosque in Istanbul, designed by Süleyman's chief architect, Sinan. Süleyman is known to the Turks as *Kanuni*, "the lawgiver," and there were great advances in the process of government under him.

During the sixteenth and seventeenth centuries, the Ottoman Empire grew by conquest, until it sprawled across North Africa, Arabia, Iraq, the Black Sea, and Ukraine, and into Europe as far as Hungary. Its advance was famously halted at the gates of Vienna in 1683, though not before the Ottomans had left their wonderful coffee behind.

Pressed back by Russian and Austrian armies, the Ottoman Empire experienced a decline in governance in the eighteenth century and neglected its foreign affairs. In the nineteenth century, it began to lose territories in the Aegean, the Balkans, North Africa, and Arabia.

The Crimean War
A brief interlude in this period of decline was the Crimean War. Regarded by Britain as a bulwark against Russian expansionism, the Ottoman Empire fought with Britain and France against the Russians in the Crimean Peninsula in 1854–56. This war was the setting for Florence Nightingale's famous hospital at Scutari (Üsküdar). In the end Russia was vanquished. The Treaty of Paris declared the Black Sea neutral, closed it to all warships, and prohibited fortifications and the presence of armaments on its shores. The independence of Turkey was affirmed and Russian influence in the area received a setback. Despite this settlement, Turkish power continued to

wane as the European powers fomented separatism among its subjects, particularly in the Balkans.

The Loss of the Balkans

Confronted by the loss of Ottoman power and turmoil in the Balkans, the young Sultan Abdülhamid II, in order to keep his critics at bay, presented a liberal constitution to a conference called by the European powers in Istanbul in 1876. The following year he retracted it and took absolute control. War broke out again in the Balkans, and Russia, which joined the insurgents, was successful everywhere. By the terms of the Treaty of San Stefano (1878) the Ottoman Empire lost most of its European possessions. Its decline was so pronounced that by the end of the century it was called "the sick man of Europe."

At home, Abdülhamid's failed promises and misgovernment led to rising discontent and pressure for change. In 1908 the group of reformers known as the "Young Turks" forced him to restore the constitution of 1876. He was deposed by a unanimous vote of parliament in 1909 and succeeded by his brother Muhammad V. From then until the outbreak of the First World War power was shared uneasily between the Sultan and the leaders of the Young Turks. In 1911–12, Tripoli (Libya) was lost to Italy. The Balkan War of 1912–13 with Greece, Serbia, and Bulgaria saw Ottoman territory in Europe reduced to an area around Adrianople and Constantinople. Because of its close economic and political links with Germany, the Ottoman Empire entered the First World War on the Kaiser's side.

The End of Empire: The Treaty of Sèvres
With the defeat of Germany in 1918 came humiliation for its Turkish ally. The Ottoman Empire was dissolved by the crushing terms of the Treaty of Sèvres, signed in 1920 with the victorious Allies (excluding Russia and the USA). The regional map was redrawn: Turkey renounced sovereignty over Mesopotamia (Iraq) and Palestine (including Transjordan), which became British mandates; Syria and Lebanon, which became French mandates; and the kingdom of Hejaz (meaning the loss of Mecca).

Perhaps the most controversial terms were those that compelled Turkey to allow Armenia to become a separate republic under international guarantees, and to see Smyrna (now Izmir) and its environs put under an interim Greek administration, with the final outcome to be decided by a vote for national self-determination by the local electorate.

In Europe, Turkey ceded parts of Eastern Thrace and certain Aegean islands to Greece, and the Dodecanese and Rhodes to Italy, retaining only Istanbul and its environs, including the neutralized and internationalized zone of the Straits. No part of Turkey was left fully independent. Turkey also had to pay reparations, enabling the Allies to tighten their control over the economy. The Treaty of Sèvres thus spelled the end of the Ottoman Empire, placed its lands in the hands of the Allies, and sparked the patriotic fire that drove Atatürk to fight for an independent Turkish nation.

Atatürk

It is worth pausing to consider the continuing impact of these events on the present day. As a visitor to Turkey you will soon recognize the face of Mustafa Kemal Atatürk, from pictures on the walls of shops, workplaces, and government buildings, and from his statue in every public square. But you  will not see cartoons of him, or hear a joke about him. Atatürk (1881–1938) is universally venerated as a visionary whose ideas changed the nation, who broke the power of the Sultan, and who created the modern Republic. Defamation of his person or character by any means is regarded as defamation of "Turkishness" and is against the law.

Mustafa Kemal (the family name Atatürk was later conferred on him by the National Assembly) was a brilliant soldier. He served as a commander in the First World War, rising to fame by repulsing the Allied assault at Gallipoli in 1915–16. This forced the Allies to retreat from European Turkey and led to the political ostracism of Winston Churchill, who had planned the campaign.

In the period between the end of the war and the announcing of the terms of the Treaty of Sèvres, the Sultan, Muhammad VI, was losing control—both to the victorious powers who were planning to carve up the Ottoman Empire and to nationalist rejection of his rule. In 1919, he sent Mustafa Kemal to crush a rebellion that had broken out in the Black Sea area

around Samsun. Instead of doing this, Mustafa
Kemal renounced his rank and titles and joined the
insurgents. Along with a number of other military
officers he established a national government at a
conference in the eastern city of Erzurum, in
opposition to the Sultan in Istanbul.

On April 23, 1920, Mustafa Kemal convened a
National Assembly in Ankara that drew up a
manifesto demanding the independence and
integrity of all parts of the Ottoman Empire
"inhabited by an Ottoman Muslim" majority. This
manifesto effectively repudiated the Treaty of Sèvres
signed by the Istanbul government. Kemal inspired
the nation to reject the postwar division of Turkey
and defy the occupying British, French, and Italian
forces. In 1921 the provisional government in
Ankara transferred political power to the people.
It formally abolished the Ottoman Sultanate, and
in 1922 the Sultan was deposed and went into exile
in Europe.

The War of Independence
In 1921 Greece ordered 100,000 troops into
Anatolia, ostensibly to support the Greeks of Izmir.
For the new Turkish nation there was no turning
back. When Atatürk launched the counteroffensive
he told his soldiers to march to the Aegean, saying
"I offer you the choice: death or the sea." The Greek
army was defeated at Dumlupınar on August 26, and
at Izmir on September 9, 1922. Izmir was destroyed.
The Turkish struggle for national sovereignty lasted
three years, and by its end the Turks had driven all
foreign forces from their land.

These victories united the nation and restored
the Turks' belief in themselves. The reconquest of
Anatolia undid the Treaty of Sèvres. Mustafa Kemal
made a separate treaty with the USSR and forced the
Allies to negotiate a new settlement. The Treaty of
Lausanne, signed in 1923, confirmed Turkey's lands
in Anatolia and removed the obligation to pay
reparations. The fate of minority populations was
a major element. The Treaty opened the way for a
large population exchange, with many hundreds of
thousands of Greeks leaving Turkey and a smaller
number of Turks leaving Greece, and secured the
rights of minorities who stayed in Turkey.

The Turkish Republic
The Turks had moved their capital from Istanbul
to remote Ankara. There, on October 29, 1923,
a secular nationalist republic was declared, and
Mustafa Kemal was unanimously elected first
President of the Republic of Turkey. The
Constitution of 1924 provided for an interim

period of one-party rule—that
of his Republican People's Party.
This allowed for a controlled
transition to full democracy.

After 1923 Mustafa Kemal
embarked on a sweeping program of Westernization
and economic development. He drove through a
series of revolutionary social and political reforms
that dealt with every aspect of the life of the people.
The Caliphate was abolished and Islam was
disestablished. Western-style dress was introduced
and the wearing of veils by women and the fez by
men was banned. The Turkish language was purged
of Arabic words and the alphabet changed from
Arabic to Latin script. Education was secularized.
Literacy programs were organized and education
for women and villagers became mandatory.
Polygamy was banned. The Gregorian calendar was
introduced, the administration overhauled, and
new legal codes introduced. The communications
infrastructure, the country's finances, and
agricultural and industrial methods were improved.

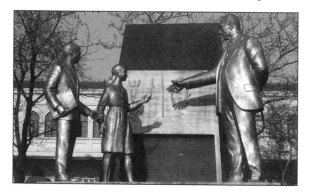

In 1934, when the use of surnames was instituted, Mustafa Kemal chose the name Atatürk, which means "Father of the Turks."

Atatürk died at the age of fifty-seven in Dolmabahçe Palace, Istanbul, on November 10, 1938. His legacy was nothing less than the transformation of Turkey from an absolute feudal monarchy into a modern, secular, sovereign state, free from foreign interference, whose citizens enjoyed greater freedom and security than their forefathers had ever known.

Modern Turkey
Atatürk was succeeded as president by his friend and colleague Ismet Inönü. Turkey was neutral through most of the Second World War, before siding with the Allies. With the development of the Cold War, steps were taken to identify with the West. In 1946 Turkey became a charter member of the United Nations. In 1950 the first free elections were held and won by the opposition Democratic Party. Great efforts were made to liberalize the economy. In 1952 Turkey joined NATO, and in 1964 it became an associate member of the European Economic Community.

Following the example of Atatürk, the Turkish army assumed a special role as protector of the Republic's secular ideals. It stood at the ready to preserve his legacy if politicians appeared to be taking steps to reverse any of his reforms. Turkey has experienced three military coups within three decades. In the late 1950s, political and economic instability caused anarchy and violence. This led to a bloodless military coup in 1960 led by General

Cemal Gürsel. In 1971 strikes and student unrest led to another coup. Military rule lasted until elections were held in 1973. The years to come were full of economic and social problems. Tension between the political left and right increased. The 1970s saw a string of coalition governments. By the end of the decade political violence had reached such a level that in 1980 another military regime was imposed by General Kenan Evren.

In 1983 there was a return to civilian rule. Turgut Özal was elected as Prime Minister, and a new constitution restructured the country to be more in line with the West. Özal and his Motherland Party focused on economic growth and further opening up Turkey to the West. Özal's reforms narrowed the political and economic gap between Turkey and Europe; he was President between 1989 and 1993.

After Turkey experienced a series of economic shocks in 2002, a major political power shift occurred, putting the religiously conservative party Adalet ve Kalkınma Partisi (AKP) in power, a position in which they remain today.

One of the key events in the AKP government's rule has been the "Ergenekon" trial, a court case involving vast numbers of military officers and other public figures accused of being members of a shadowy "deep-state" organization that committed political assassinations and various other crimes in order to thwart the democratic process. Opinion is divided in Turkey as to the veracity of these accusations. The Ergenekon investigation began after a number of high-profile murders, including that of Armenian journalist Hrant Dink and three Christian missionaries in Malatya. It has also involved the exhumation of the body of President Özal on suspicion that he had been poisoned.

One result of the ongoing Ergenekon investigation and trial is that the power of the military in Turkish politics has been significantly curtailed. As a result of court rulings in 2013 many army officers, including generals, are now serving prison sentences.

The AKP has also been responsible for a major effort to bring the decades-long conflict in the Kurdish-dominated southeast to an end. Talks have begun with the Kurdish separatist, terrorist, PKK organization, and many terrorists have begun to lay down their arms. The chance for peace is better than it has been for many years.

However, not all parts of Turkish society are supportive of the AKP. Prime Minister Recep Tayyip Erdoğan is accused by his opponents of being dictatorial, which led to major protests across Turkey in early summer 2013. The country is now polarized between secularists who support Atatürk's social

revolution and those who believe in more traditional, conservative Islamic values. The laws are gradually becoming more relaxed about the wearing of headscarves in the public arena.

A Constitutional Committee has been set up with the aim of rewriting the Constitution, the current one dating from the era just after the last military coup. The eyes of both government supporters and protesters are on this project.

ATTITUDES TO HISTORY

Attitudes to history are changing in Turkey. With the foundation of the Republic, a break was made with the Ottoman past. The focus of the nation's life was moved from Ottoman Istanbul to republican Ankara. The modern period was perceived as very much better than the old. Today, with the reduction in the political and social power of secularists, there is a growing interest in all things Ottoman. A major popular television serial is called "Magnificent Century" and focuses on the life and times of Süleyman the Magnificent. Some government functions are moving back to Istanbul, and history professors are beginning to focus more on the Ottoman period than ever before.

The Turkish People Today

Owing to a high birthrate and traditionally poor health care, the Turks are a very young nation by Western standards. You will see young people everywhere, and this gives the country great dynamism and an enterprising spirit. It is astonishing to realize that only 7.5 percent of the Turkish population are over sixty-five!

Eighty percent of the population are ethnic Turks; 18 percent are Kurds; other ethnic groups include the Laz people in the Black Sea region, Christian minorities (Armenians, Greeks, Assyrians, Suryani), and Jews.

Ever since the founding of the Republic the Turkish government has downplayed ethnic, linguistic, and religious distinctions, fearful that a divided country could become the scene of ethnic violence and civil war. Thus the 1965 census was the last one to list linguistic minorities.

The Kurds, the country's largest minority, have posed the most serious and persistent challenge to national unity. Kurdish people traditionally have lived in an area encompassing southeastern Turkey and northern Iraq. The Turkish state has always sought to minimize the differences between Turks and Kurds, often describing the latter as "mountain Turks," and its policies have received both the approval (for citizenship, education for all, etc.) and disapproval (for limitations on the use of the Kurdish language, etc.) of the West.

The greatest fear of the Turks is that Kurdish nationalism will result in secession, similar to that seen in the former Yugoslavia in the late twentieth century, and the breakup of their state. Many Kurdish people have assimilated into Turkish society and are successful businessmen, and in recent years there have even been prominent politicians of

Kurdish origin. However, radical Kurdish groups have taken up arms in the southeast, and perpetrated terrorist acts in Turkey's major cities. The most well-known Kurdish terror group was the PKK. Since a ceasefire in the late 1990s and the capture and conviction of the PKK leader, there has been relative peace in the region.

As part of the process of adapting to the requirements of the European Union, greater rights have been granted to minorities, such as broadcasts in the Kurdish language, but change is gradual. Many Turks still fear that foreign powers wish to encourage Kurdish nationalism, and keep a wary eye on the development of Kurdish autonomy in neighboring Iraq.

A foreign visitor in Turkey would be well advised not to take sides in the debate on nationalism, or to voice opinions about certain events in Turkey's past, such as the sensitive issue of whether or not there was an Armenian massacre. All Turkish schoolchildren are taught about the Treaty of Sèvres and the attempted partition of Turkey by the victorious Allies, and about the encouragement given to seditious and often violent minority groups at that time. Turks are sensitive, almost to the point of paranoia, to the possibility that foreign powers might still wish to destabilize the country through the promotion of nationalism among ethnic minorities. One right-wing political party regularly uses the slogan "Our land is an indivisible whole." Beware of political debate: it will lose you friends and could result in a run-in with the authorities.

TURKISH CITIES
Istanbul

Few cities can rival Istanbul's fascinating mix of culture and history. It has been the capital of empires and for nearly 1,500 years stood at the pivot of world history. The silhouette of its skyline viewed from the Bosporus is breathtakingly beautiful, and visitors are dazzled by the richness of its cultural heritage. Istanbul is the economic powerhouse of Turkey. As real estate prices increase, there is a trend toward building taller tower blocks, for both office and residential use.

Istanbul today spreads across both the Asian and European shores of the Bosporus. A ceaseless flood of migrants from rural Anatolia has swollen the population, forming the largest city in Turkey. The population figure in the 2012 census was over 13.8 million, but unofficial estimates put it as high as 18 million. European Istanbul contains the historic and business heart of the city. Asian Istanbul is more residential and better laid out. The two sides are linked by two large suspension bridges, and a multitude of ferries and boats. In 2013 the rail link under the Bosporus, the Marmaray project, was due to open and construction of a third bridge across the

Bosporus has begun. High-rise apartment complexes
line both coasts as far as the eye can see. Around
both parts of the city there is an unregulated jumble
of housing built by migrants from the countryside;
out-of-town satellite luxury developments of villas
and apartments are also springing up.

Istanbul is no longer the political capital of
Turkey, but it is the cultural and economic center,
and the commercial hub of the country. High-rise
office complexes, shopping malls, and modern art
galleries abut ancient monuments and museums
and galleries housing the treasures of former ages.
The embassies are in Ankara, but many consulates
service Istanbul. The AK government has
designated part of the Asian side of Istanbul as a
financial services center, including a controversial
decision to move the Central Bank from Ankara
to this new office development.

A growing city, Istanbul is rapidly trying to
develop its infrastructure to keep pace with its
burgeoning population. Construction is underway
everywhere. One visitor was heard to exclaim,
"Istanbul will be great once it is finished!"

Ankara
The capital, Ankara has experienced phenomenal
growth in recent years. It is the seat of government
and of all of the ministries, and is the second-largest
city, with a population of just over 4.8 million. It
was home to Atatürk after he became leader of the
movement for a free state, and has been the capital
since 1923. Before then it was a sleepy Anatolian
village, famous for the angora (Ankara) goat.

Ankara is situated on a plateau 3,000 feet (914 meters) above sea level. The rapid growth of the city and resultant increase in traffic has created a smog problem, which in recent years has been relieved to some extent. Ankara is a city of bureaucrats, overshadowed by the expansive and cosmopolitan city of Istanbul, and remains in a way more provincial. It is well laid out with wide boulevards, parks, and public amenities. Foreign embassies are located here. There is a friendly rivalry between the business elite of Istanbul and their bureaucratic masters in Ankara: many Istanbulites maintain that the best thing about Ankara is the road back to Istanbul.

Izmir
Turkey's third-largest city, with a population of over 3.6 million, is Izmir, the pearl of the Aegean. It has been a major port since biblical times, when it was known as Smyrna. Today it is home to an important NATO naval base, as well as to an annual trade fair. In the late twentieth century Izmir regained its status as a "pearl" when the bay, which had become known for its stench, was cleaned up. The promenade is lined with cafés and there is a real Western feel to the city. Many of the figs eaten in England at Christmas will have come from Izmir. It is also a major tobacco producer.

GOVERNMENT
Turkey is one of the few Muslim nations to have a true parliamentary democracy. Based on the 1982

constitution, it is a democratic, secular, parliamentary republic. Its legislature, executive, and judiciary are independent of each other.

The head of state is the president. He, or she, is elected by the members of the Grand National Assembly (parliament) and serves a term of seven years. The president represents the "integrity of the Turkish Republic and the Turkish nation" and is nonpartisan. The president does not set the political agenda or lead the government: this is done by the prime minister and the Council of Ministers (cabinet). However, the president can veto laws passed by the parliament. The president also ensures that the constitution is not violated, and that the government functions properly.

The unicameral Grand National Assembly is democratically elected. Its 450 deputies serve a five-year term. The leader of the party that wins the most seats is appointed prime minister. Some readers may be surprised to learn that Turkish law is not based on Islamic, or Sharia, law. It is based on the Swiss code, which means that an act is illegal until specifically enabled by a body of law.

Before an election the streets are covered in banners bearing the logos of political parties, and vans and buses drive around with loudspeakers blaring out lively music and promises for change. Often there are more than ten parties campaigning at one time. The parties range from conservative nationalists and fundamentalist Islamists on the right to the far left. They are always changing because of internal differences and power struggles. Parties often split and give rise to new ones.

Sometimes they are shut down for illegal activities, and the same faces resurface later in a new party with a new name.

The judiciary is independent. The courts include the Constitutional Court, the Supreme Court of Appeals, the Council of State, the Supreme Council of Public Accounts, the Supreme Military Administrative Tribunal, the Military Court of Appeal, the Court of Jurisdictional Disputes, and the Supreme Electoral Board.

The Role of the Army
Turkish sovereignty is vested in parliament, but, as we have seen, the army has an important role as the guarantor of Atatürk's republic. A National Security Council meets regularly, headed by the president and attended by government ministers and senior officers in the armed services. According to the present constitution, if the military feels that the government has acted in an unconstitutional way, it is allowed to step in. After the military coup on

September 12, 1980, the general public was relieved. Why? Because the military restored civil, fiscal, and legal order and enacted the 1982 Constitution defining the government's powers. The military's presence in national affairs has often been viewed

with suspicion by the West, but it is probably one of the main reasons Turkey is a democratic Islamic nation. It was always Turkey's secular circles that pushed and encouraged the military to stage coups, seeing the army as an important counterbalance to elements that would prefer a more Islamic form of government and law.

On February 28, 1997 (known as the "Postmodern" coup) at the National Security Council (MGK) meeting the generals submitted their views on issues regarding secularism and political Islam in Turkey to the government. The MGK made several decisions during this meeting, and the Prime Minister, Necmettin Erbakan from the Welfare Party, was forced to sign the decisions intending to protect the secularist ideology in Turkey.

However, the recent Ergenekon case has severely weakened the Turkish army's role in political life

Local Government
There are eighty-one provinces, divided into municipalities and villages. Every province has a

governor, responsible for the departments of law enforcement, education, and citizenship. First-time visitors to Turkey are often surprised by the visible presence of police force and tanks. The police monitor cities and towns, the gendarmes (military police) the rural areas. The municipality supervises the fire department, local transportation, public amenities, and refuse collection.

THE ECONOMY

When Atatürk came to power the economy was mainly agricultural and most people lived in rural areas. Atatürk led a drive for modernization, and the early Republican era had an air of enterprise. New industries were founded. These included state-owned manufacturing and service companies such as tobacco- or sugar-processing plants, oil refineries, iron and steel factories, banks, and insurance companies. Turkey has made progress and today has a mixed economy with a strong tertiary sector (banking, finance, computers, consulting, etc.), a manufacturing base (in particular, textiles, and car manufacture), and agricultural and other raw material industries (such as cotton, marble, tobacco, citrus fruits, wheat).

Turkey has become the breadbasket of the Middle East. It exports perishable items to Europe and the USA as well as to its neighbors. It is one of the world's main providers of hazelnuts, pistachios, and textiles. Turkish construction, transportation, and engineering companies are active in the Middle East and Central Asia.

During the 1980s and 1990s the economy was stagnant. Inflation soared (up to three figures), and Turks suffered under the drastic corrective devaluation of the Turkish Lira (TL). However, the large government deficit has been funded by national and international debt, and since 2002 the market has stabilized and inflation has fallen. Turkey's economy is now strong, with credit

rating agencies in 2013 upgrading the country to "investment grade." Cities in Anatolia are booming— under the AKP government Turkey has seen the rise of so-called "green capital companies," green being the color of conservative Islam. Many retail and industrial companies have sprung up with this type of ownership, and Islamic-style banking is now becoming available in Turkey.

RELATIONS WITH THE WEST

Turkey has always been influenced by both East and West. Today, paradoxically, it is at the same time a profoundly Muslim society and a modern Western state. It is a member of the United Nations, the Organization for Economic Cooperation and Development, the North Atlantic Treaty Organization, and the Islamic Conference, and is still hoping to join the European Union.

Before the fall of Communism and the breakup of the Soviet Union, Turkey was of great strategic importance to the West as it formed the eastern boundary of NATO. A NATO fleet was based in Izmir, and the airbases of

Adana and Batman, and Istanbul (guarding the Bosporus and access to the Black Sea), were vital strategic assets.

With the transition from the Cold War to the War on Terror, Turkey has again become an important strategic partner. As one of the few truly democratic Islamic nations, it is viewed by many as a model for outward-looking Islam, and an example of peaceful coexistence between the Christian and Muslim worlds. At the same time, the West recognizes Turkey's strong cultural links with Central Asia and the Islamic world, and that there are elements in Turkish society that would like it to reduce its ties with the West and increase those with the Middle East and Central Asia.

Turkey's large Muslim population means it is often feared by the West and wooed at the same time. Nowhere is this more evident than in the response to Turkey's application to join the European Union. Turkey was given a number of conditions to fulfill, dealing with areas as diverse as the economy and human rights. These are known as the Copenhagen criteria. The period since the defining of these criteria has been marked by some progress having been made toward these goals, with Turks feeling they are receiving very little in return in the way of movement toward accession. Many are beginning to wonder if Turkey should instead aim to be a regional power and turn its eyes eastward.

CYPRUS

The issue of the divided island republic of Cyprus, and the related dispute between Greece and Turkey, is a major obstacle to Turkey's efforts to join the EU. The island has been fought over for centuries, but the present crisis has its roots in the 1960s. The population of Cyprus is a mix of Muslim Turks and Orthodox Greeks. In the latter half of the twentieth century, by the terms of the 1959 Treaty of London, Britain, Greece, and Turkey shared political responsibility for the stability and security of Cyprus. During the 1960s tension between the two communities increased, with killings and bloody reprisals. The Turkish minority felt underrepresented and feared that the Greek majority wanted Cyprus to join Greece.

Increased intercommunal violence and a coup by extreme right-wing Greek officers of the Cypriot National Guard against the government of President Makarios led Turkish Prime Minister Bülent Ecevıt to send troops into Cyprus in 1974. Turkey considered itself to be acting in accordance with the Treaty of London, in defense of Turkish Cypriot lives and liberty. The Western world saw this act as an invasion. Stalemate on the ground led to the division of the island into two parts separated by a demilitarized zone. The northern, Turkish part declared itself the Turkish Federated State of Cyprus, and was recognized by Turkey. The rest of the world regarded the new state as illegitimate, and only recognized the government of the southern, Greek part.

Despite various attempts to reach a political settlement on the island, the old enmity between Greeks and Turks continues. In 2004 a referendum was held on the question of reuniting the island. In a reversal of their previously entrenched positions, the Turkish population voted "yes" to unification and the Greek population voted "no." The inclusion of Cyprus in the EU has caused more political difficulties than it has solved, and the issue of a divided Cyprus looks set to remain for some time.

chapter **two**

VALUES &
ATTITUDES

A POLARIZED SOCIETY

Today Turkish society is extremely polarized along
the lines of religion. Social commentators stress the
division between those whose attitudes and values
are secular, and those whose are Islamic. It is
therefore hard to give general descriptions that
cover both halves of Turkish society.

Clashes of culture and debates between these
two viewpoints dominate the social and political
scene. In early 2013 the argument over what is
Turkey's national drink raged for days after the
Prime Minister said it should be the yogurt-based
"ayran" rather than the alcoholic drink "rakı."

Beyond the religious divide, however, there are
deep underlying values shared by all Turks.

RESPECT AND HONOR

Turkish culture places great emphasis on respect,
honor, and pride. This is a society where "old-
fashioned" manners are still practiced to some
degree. University students and young adults tend
to be less formal. Last names are rarely used; instead,
titles are applied to the first name as signs of respect
or relationship. It is rude to call a new acquaintance

by his or her first name only. It is polite, depending on the situation, to use either *amca* or *teyze* (uncle or aunt), or *bey* or *hanım* (sir or madam), after the person's first name. A young adult will be addressed by children and youth as *abla* (elder sister) or *ağabey* (big brother), alone or after their given name. Others may respectfully call you *abla*, *ağabey*, *teyze*, or *amca*. If you are an instructor, educator, or teacher, you may be called by your first name followed by *hoca* (teacher), pronounced "hodja." If you are an expert in a particular field you may be called by your first name followed by *usta* (expert).

Seniority is owed considerable respect in Turkey; young people will pay visits to their elders on special holidays first, and will be actively concerned with their well-being. More recently those who can afford it may travel abroad during official holidays rather than spend the time with extended family. It is not unusual to see someone making a gesture such as a gentle bow when greeting someone senior to themselves in either age or authority. Gray-haired visitors may find themselves treated especially well.

Honor is important and Turkish culture is strongly hierarchical and patriarchal. Individuals are ranked according to status. Age is significant in determining this. Determining relative status by age, however, also depends on the older person's perception of himself. A visitor in his twenties who, with honorable intentions, addresses a man in his forties as "uncle," when that man may prefer to be called "brother," may elicit some teasing from his friends, but the general rule is that until the foreigner knows how a person wishes to be treated, he should show more honor rather than less. It is better to err on the conservative side.

Showing Respect
Showing respect is vital. Other people who are normally honored may have power based on individual reputation, family, fame, wealth, and political or religious leadership. Also, people in positions of authority will be honored by those under them; for example, an employer will be treated deferentially by an employee, and a teacher will be honored by a student.

It is important to know how and when to honor others. A visitor, particularly from a Western background, can easily fail to observe ways of affirming status. For example, you should not turn your back on a person of importance. This may be deeply insulting for the person of special status. You are expected to back away. A visitor who does not behave with due deference is considered rude.

Many Turks smoke a lot. However, they will not do so in front of an older person, as a sign of respect. Do not be surprised if someone leaves the room for a few minutes to smoke a cigarette.

Another area of honor is related to the family. The family's good name depends much on the honor and modesty of the women and their virtuous behavior and/or the family's economic status. Loss of face can be detrimental to relatives. If honor is questioned and the family's reputation is damaged, family members are responsible for restoring the family's honor by ostracizing the member in question. A Turkish proverb that illustrates how an outsider should respond in such a situation says it all: "Do not speak of rope in the house of a hanged man."

The general rule is: when unsure, say nothing. Turks feel that it is impolite to speak as directly as some foreigners do. Frankness and honesty are not always seen as positive attributes. In cases where they challenge a harmonious relationship, they are negative. Harmony is more important than being open. If directness causes someone to lose face and makes him feel that his feelings are not valued, he may not forget or forgive. It is also possible that others may be affected, and will not forget it or forgive him. A person who feels insulted may hold a grudge for a lifetime.

Turks generally appear very confident. In order to save face, it is common not to admit to a weakness or mistake. Shifting blame is expected. Self-disclosure happens only with close friends.

Dignity
Dignity, not to be confused with honor, but as important, should always be preserved. For example, a request for a substantial favor will be made indirectly or by a third party. Visitors who are used to more directness must learn not to give straight refusals or a frank "no." Such a direct reply would cause the person who has made the request to lose face. It is best to give an answer that causes no embarrassment to either party. If rejecting the request, it is advisable to put the blame on an outside cause, and avoid possible personal offense.

You may think of this, or of the use of a third party in making a request, as being manipulative. Or, as a Westerner who values frankness and directness, you could interpret polite and indirect answers as being dishonest. But you should understand that this is not so for your Turkish friend. These are examples of different viewpoints leading to cultural clashes between Turks and Westerners.

FAMILY, FRIENDS, COMMUNITY

Turkish society is very group-oriented. Group allegiance is paramount, and Turks will be faithful to the group on which they depend for their identity and support. An idiom to affirm this is "In the end, you know who your family is." It is a multifaceted value found in each level of society.

The social unit with the strongest demands on a person's loyalty is the family—the fundamental structure of life. It gives many benefits but requires certain obligations. A Turkish proverb goes "A sheep separated from the flock is eaten by wolves." The family expects deep loyalty in all aspects of life, social and otherwise. The eldest son always has a special place of responsibility, helping his father and caring for younger siblings in his father's absence. Children are treated with special indulgence when they are young. When they are grown they are truly a kind of social security for their parents. The family will naturally help each other in difficult circumstances, whether or not these are of the member's own making—for example, an older

sister who works may support a younger brother
who is unemployed.

Friends are also important. Friendship may
involve great commitment and mutual concern,
and a lot of time. To establish a true friendship
takes effort. It is important to visit regularly and
to help in times of need. Friends never betray one
another. Friendships are formed for many reasons,
one of them being expectation of mutual help. If a
favor is done for someone, that person and usually
his family will be obligated to remember it.

Turkish people generally form friendships with
others of the same sex, who are of a similar age and
status. Usually, unequal economic or social status
precludes deep friendship. If a man and woman
are friends, they will refer to each other in kinship
terms; for example, a woman would consider her
husband's friend to be like her *kardeş* (brother)
and not her *dost* (friend), which would imply an
improperly familiar or possibly romantic
relationship.

Community is highly valued. Neighbors and relatives help each other in many practical ways, such as providing food or beds for each other's guests. If a crisis occurs, the support of community and neighbors is usually strong. Action arising from group affiliation rather than individualism is common.

NATIONAL PRIDE

The Turkish phrase, "*Ne mutlu Türküm diyene!*" ("How happy is he or she who can say, I am Turkish!") is one of the most frequently encountered slogans. This expression genuinely reflects most Turkish people's belief in and commitment to their nation and homeland.

Mustafa Kemal Atatürk restored to the Turks pride in their nationality and homeland. This is deep-seated, and expresses itself in some surprising ways—for example, it is an offense to wear a garment made out of the flag. A beloved TV presenter outraged the national press recently by kicking a balloon that had the crescent and star on it during a program celebrating Republic Day. It is a serious insult to make jokes about the national anthem, the flag, or Atatürk. Turks may be critical of their own nation or government, but they will not like it if you agree with them or make negative statements yourself.

The extreme face of national pride can be seen in right-wing parties such as the MHP (Nationalist Action Party), which, with its slogan of "Turkey for the Turks," is typically anti-Western and anti-foreigner. MHP supporters often meet in clubs called *Ülkü Ocağı* (fraternities of principle). These *Ülkü Ocağı* are symbolized by a wolf and the crescent and star, and supporters at political rallies may make a hand sign portraying a wolf.

ATATÜRK, SECULARISM, AND RELIGION

Although Atatürk, in a complete break with the past, established a secular government, Islam continues to have a pivotal role in the life and character of the nation.

Turkish society can be broadly divided into four subgroups: Atatürk supporters (secularists), Leftists, Islamic fundamentalists, and modern Islamists.

Atatürk supporters uphold links with the West and look for modernization at every opportunity. They are educated, middle-class, progressive citizens who are Muslim. They oppose Islamic law and believe it is backward and dangerous. They revere Atatürk, and often can be heard to mourn that there is no one like him today. They are fiercely loyal to the values of democracy, liberalization, and modernization stressed by him.

Atatürk supporters wear lapel pins bearing his image, visit the Anıtkabir (his mausoleum in Ankara), quote his speeches, and display his picture. His picture hangs in most public buildings. Many important public places such as dams, airports, and roadways are named after him. Evidence of Kemal Atatürk is everywhere, and first-time visitors to Turkey may mistakenly equate this with the leadership cult of former communist countries. However, veneration of Atatürk, while encouraged by the school system, is not imposed by the government.

The second subgroup is known as Muslim Socialists. The followers are Turks of leftist persuasion who are anti-Western and not devout Muslims. The two leftist Muslim groups are the Revolutionary Muslims and Anti-Capitalist Muslims.

The third subgroup is the Islamic fundamentalists. They are fiercely opposed to the followers of Atatürk. They wish to see the nation return to Islamic values and believe the five pillars of Islam and Islamic law should be diligently practiced. They reject the notion of a secular state and would support, to varying degrees, integration of state and religion, even to the extent of the imposition of Sharia law. They promote activities disliked by the secularists such as the wearing of headscarves and the teaching of Arabic and the Koran to children.

The fourth subgroup is modern Islamists. This recently formed grouping consists of well-educated, middle-class individuals who are Islamic rather than secular. The women wear headscarves. Modern Islamists oppose alcohol, clubs, and provocative dress such as miniskirts and low-cut party dresses. In a social setting they tend to separate men and women. Their use of language is influenced by Islamic terminology and Ottoman Turkish, Arabic, and Persian loan words. They tend to do business within their own network. Modern

Islamists support the AK Party, which, while attempting to lessen the separation of state and religion, still seeks closer links with the West. An important grass roots organization among the modern Islamists is the "Hizmet" group, with its links to the Turkish Muslim teacher Fethullah Gülen who lives in America. The group is linked with schools, businesses, and media conglomerates in Turkey.

THE FIVE PILLARS OF ISLAM

- The creed, called *shahada* (meaning testimony or witness): if a person recites "There is no god but Allah and Muhammad is his prophet" he will be considered a Muslim.
- Prayer five times a day.
- Observation of the annual fast during the month of Ramadan.
- Giving of alms.
- The Hajj: every Muslim should plan to make the pilgrimage to Mecca at least once during his or her lifetime.

ISLAM

"To be a Turk is to be a Muslim" is a statement that defines both nationality and culture. More than 99 percent of the population are Muslim, although they may not be practicing Muslims.

The most noticeable sign of Islam for the visitor is the call to prayer (*ezan*) that echoes across Turkey's villages and towns five times a day. The times of prayer are sunrise, noon, mid-afternoon, sunset, and late night. The call is in Arabic and starts with the statement "*Allah-u Akbar,*" which means, "God is great."

Often the prayer calls at different mosques start just seconds or minutes after each other, so they form a chorus around the city. The call to prayer is given by a *muezzin*, who is specially trained in the melody of the chant. The *muezzin* used to have to climb stairs to the top of the minaret. With the convenience of technology, the *muezzin* may now sit below and use a microphone and loudspeakers.

Islam is both a faith and a way of life, an integral belief system that is both religious and political. The one God, Allah, is recognized as the creator of everything in the universe. He is the ultimate source of *ruh* (life spirit).

The Koran is the holy book of Islam. It is understood to be the written word of God as revealed to the Prophet Muhammad, who recited the chapters (or *suras*) of the Koran to scribes for notation. The Koran is sacred and is considered one of the most beautiful works in Arabic literature. Many Muslim traditions and practices are contained not in the Koran, but in the Hadith: a written record of what the Prophet Muhammad said, did, or approved.

The mosque is the primary community space for Islamic teaching and religious activity. The *imam* is both prayer leader and teacher at the mosque. The majority of Turkish Muslims are from the mainstream Sunni tradition. Among the well-known smaller groups or sects present in Turkey are the Sufis and Alevis. Both groups appreciate and use music as part of their worship, and their beliefs include mysticism.

The Alevis, who are Shiites, comprise about 20 percent of the population. They differ from Sunnis in that they believe the line of the Caliphate goes through Ali, the cousin and son-in-law of the Prophet Muhammad. Instead of the mosque, they worship and meet in the *cemevi*, or community hall. They are more like a society or religious association. Men and women are permitted to sit in the same *cemevi*, although they are segregated. Meals, music, dances, and sometimes alcohol are part of their communal worship. Their leaders are known as *pir* (spiritual leader) and *dede* (a senior Dervish in the Alevi sect, similar to an elder).

NEW RELIGIOUS STRUCTURES
Turkish Islam used to be centrally led by the Sultan in his capacity as Caliph, spiritual leader of all Muslims. The caliphate was abolished by Atatürk, but the state still oversees religious affairs.

The Turkish state directs and supervises the expression and interpretation of religion. The Department of Religious Affairs is a government body, under the authority of the prime minister. Article 136 of the Turkish constitution established this department to oversee the principles of belief, worship, and moral standards in Turkey "in accordance with the principles of a secular State, separate from any political ideology and in accordance with the principle of national unity." The department appoints and trains all religious leaders. A Muslim scholar, or *mufti*, is appointed head in each province and county; this individual oversees all the *imams* and rules on points of observance, in accordance with the principles laid down by the Department of Religious Affairs.

All religious education is given either through Koran schools licensed by the Department of Religious Affairs, or through the state education system (schools and universities) run by the Department of National Education.

Questions of Islamic practice are settled with reference to the Department of Religious Affairs, and their Web site provides details on the daily times for the call to prayer, a verse and Hadith saying for the day, and the opportunity to e-mail your religious questions to an expert.

EDUCATION

Urban middle- and upper-class Turks place great importance on education. Parents encourage their children to work hard and do well in order to secure a well-paid job in the future. In the past the majority of women who attended university went for two reasons: to find someone of equal social standing to marry, and to gain a degree for a career. A recent trend is that more women are graduating and entering the professional sector.

Children must attend school for eight years, beginning at the age of six. There are two types of schools: private and public. Public schools have exceptionally large classes. Kindergarten (*yuva*) and preschool (*anaokul*) are always private.

Education is controlled by the National Ministry of Education (Milli Eğitim Bakanlığı). The elementary school week begins and ends with the national anthem, and daily the children promise to uphold Atatürk's principles, chanting "I am a Turk, I am right, I am hard-working. My guiding principles are to protect those weaker than me, to respect my elders and to love my land and my nation more than I love myself. My country is on the ascent and advancing. O, great Atatürk, I swear that I will constantly walk in the way which you created for me and toward the goal which you showed me. May my whole being be a gift to the Turkish nation. How blessed is he who can say, 'I am a Turk.'"

The number of private schools and universities has increased significantly in recent years, causing the education system to undergo many changes.

For decades students learned by rote. However, there has been a gradual move toward a more experimental approach. Turkish schools tend to be strong on math, Turkish language, history, religion, and citizenship. Competition to pass entrance exams for high schools and university is fierce. The system has developed in such a way that children have to take additional special courses at private colleges, or *dershanes*, to prepare them for these exams. Turkish children have a lot of homework and take extra classes on the weekend. Parents often put great pressure on them to gain better marks for acceptance in schools where lessons are taught in German, English, or French.

Many universities teach in foreign languages and offer two- and four-year degree programs.

THE ROLE OF WOMEN

The role of women has changed drastically over the centuries. As the level of education increases, the idea that women are important only for serving men's needs and for childbearing is diminishing. Topkapı Palace with its sultan's harem is now just a tourist site. As you walk down the street you can see a mix of women, from those in headscarves projecting an image of subservience to men, to miniskirted office employees relaxing in a sushi bar after work. Women drive privately owned cars—but we have yet to see a woman driving a taxi, truck, or bus! They run companies. They are top models,

TV presenters, and politicians. In the 1990s, Turkey had a female prime minister.

The civil code enacted in 1926 abolished polygamy and introduced a minimum age for marriage. It also gave equality of inheritance and made a woman's testimony as valid as a man's in a court of law. Atatürk gave women the right to vote in 1930—earlier than in many European countries.

Promotion is often readily available on merit for women working in industry and offices. The glass ceiling so often complained of elsewhere in Europe is less in evidence in the modern Turkish company. Educated middle- and upper-class women fill many important roles in professional fields such as finance, law, and medicine.

Some Turkish women define their roles in domestic terms, as a good mother and wife. In towns, villages, or lower-class areas, many women would describe their main role as that of tension manager in the home. The mother is the person to whom all have access, acting as mediator between father and children and generally attempting to ease the strains created by social change.

The importance of a woman maintaining her honor is crucial. It is believed that proper behavior between men and women depends most of all on the woman. Chastity is taken very seriously. In some respects, the standard for men is not the same for women. Improper behavior can result in family ostracism or even more serious action, such as a decision by the family elders to appoint a male relative as summary executioner.

Although things are gradually changing, particularly for educated women, some traditional rules still apply: for example, if a woman has to live alone for any period of time, a female relative will join her or she will be invited to a relative's home. A woman living on her own is unusual.

In general, when in public, a woman's movements should be reserved and careful, and in social settings she should be restrained and avoid friendly smiles, eye contact, and casual friendliness in mixed company. In a work context this may vary, depending on the situation and status of the people involved.

MEMLEKET AND HEMŞEHRI
The concepts of hometown, *memleket,* and fellow countrymen, *hemşehri,* are strong. Even with the tremendous migration to towns and cities, Turks

rarely lose their ties with the past. People who have been born in an urban center may choose to identify themselves as being from a different place—the place where their family roots are. The words of a Turkish song capture this loyalty and identity perfectly: "There is a village far away; whether we go there or not it is still our village."

People have a sense of loyalty toward those who are from the same area. Social clubs exist in most of the big cities where people from a particular region can meet. These associations are important for mutual help and support. It is very common for small businesses such as restaurants to mention the name of the area they have come from in the name of the business.

chapter three

CUSTOMS &
TRADITIONS

NATIONAL HOLIDAYS

Turkey seems to have many national holidays, but if one falls on a weekend a working day is not given in lieu. The Turkish official calendar is the Western Gregorian one and the nonreligious national holidays are on fixed dates, many of which commemorate a significant event in the Atatürk era. The religious holidays are based on the Muslim lunar calendar and so their dates change each year. During most holidays many people travel, either to see their family in other parts of the country or to take a vacation in Turkey or abroad. Intercity buses and air flights are fully booked weeks in advance. The roads are crowded and many accidents occur.

New Year's Day: January 1

While fundamentalist Muslims believe it is a sin to celebrate this holiday, secular Muslim Turks do not. It is celebrated as Christmas is celebrated in Europe and America, with most of the same trimmings. After all, Father Christmas is based on Saint Nicholas, who came from the Myra/Antalya region of Turkey. Christmas trees and decorations are put up, and families exchange presents and have a

turkey dinner on New Year's Eve. Generally an
appropriate business gift is a New Year's basket,
with food items such as chocolate, coffee, cheese,
fruit, and even alcohol or a pack of cigarettes
(depending on where the recipient stands on the
secular/Islamic polemic!).

Çocuk Bayramı: April 23

National Sovereignty and Children's Day
commemorates the day that Atatürk convened
the Grand National Assembly during the War of
Independence. Every school has a special ceremony
and parades, and poems about Atatürk are recited.
Also, children from around the world are flown to
Ankara to participate in an international and
national folklore ceremony.

Everyone hangs out flags, and government
offices have huge flags or a picture of Atatürk
draped over them. Officials visit the Anıtkabir
mausoleum in Ankara, where Atatürk is buried,
and similar ceremonies are held at the Atatürk
statue in each city. Buy a few sweets—children
will probably be ringing your doorbell!

Gençlik Bayramı: May 19

Youth and Sport Day commemorates Atatürk's landing in Samsun to organize the revolution and start the War of Independence. Every sports arena hosts a parade of young people, with folk dancing, sporting displays, and speeches. Ceremonies take place in town squares. There is a huge celebration in the city of Samsun, where a whole neighborhood and also the university are called "19th May."

Zafer Bayramı: August 30

This commemorates the victory in the War of Independence, when foreign powers were expelled from Turkish soil. A military parade is held in Ankara, and in Istanbul navy and helicopter fleets display along the Bosporus. Ceremonies are held at the statue of Atatürk in every city and dignitaries visit the Anıtkabir. Civic parades are held in the evening, often by torchlight, along main streets.

Cumhüriyet Bayramı: October 29

This is the anniversary of the day the Republic was founded. It is the biggest event in the year for flags

and for ceremonies commemorating Atatürk and the Republic.

November 10
This is not a holiday, but there is a minute of silence at 9:05 a.m. to mark the anniversary of the passing of Atatürk. If you are in public, stop what you are doing, and stand to attention in silence. Fire alarms and sirens will go off, and drivers will hoot their horns. In recent years participation in this commemoration has been less than 100 percent as those with a more Islamic worldview have begun to question some of Atatürk's legacy.

RELIGIOUS HOLIDAYS
These change each year in line with the Muslim calendar. The lunar calendar is about eleven days shorter than the Gregorian one, so the holidays move forward each year. The dates are officially declared after astronomers have made the

necessary observations and calculations. The civil authorities then determine how many days the civil holiday should last. If the timing means that there is just one working day between the weekend and the holiday, it may be decided to join the two together and make one long week of holiday.

Feast of Sacrifice (*Kurban Bayramı: Eid al-Adha*)
This is the most important religious holiday of the year. It lasts for four days and commemorates the Koranic story in which the patriarch Abraham shows the ultimate act of submission to the will of Allah (*Islam* means "submission") by being prepared to sacrifice his son. God stops him and instead leads him to sacrifice a ram. (This is similar to the biblical account, except that in Islam the son is Ishmael, not Isaac.)

The story is commemorated by the sacrifice of an animal on the first day of the holiday, immediately after morning prayer. Recent changes in public health laws mean it is illegal for people to sacrifice an animal in their backyard—the municipality provides locations for livestock purchase and for professionals to carry out the sacrifices. The meat is given to the poor and needy, and shared with neighbors and friends.

Ramadan
This holy month of fasting is referred to as "sultan (king) of the other eleven months." It is a mandatory fast; individuals can also voluntarily fast at other times of the year. Good Muslims abstain from food, drink, sex, and smoking during the

hours of daylight. These depend on the time of year: in the winter the days are shorter, so the fast is easier than when it occurs in summer. Calendars are printed showing the exact times at which the fast begins in the morning and ends in the evening. These times vary from city to city across Turkey: Istanbul and Izmir in the west will fast after Trabzon and Diyarbakır in the east. Children, travelers, pregnant women, and the sick are exempt. A lot of preparation is necessary: women clean their houses from top to bottom and fully stock their larders for the traditional meals.

People who are fasting can get up early before sunrise for a meal called *sahur*. Drummers go up and down the street beating drums as a warning that the sun is about to rise, and that it is the last chance to eat before daylight. At the end of the month, the drummers ring every doorbell, expecting to get a tip.

Each day the fast is broken at sundown. The breaking of the fast, called *iftar*, begins with a prayer. It is tradition to have a date or olive to start (Muhammad traditionally used dates). There are many ways of knowing when the right moment has arrived. The "*Ramazan topu*" used to be a live cannon or shot fired from the mosque; it has now been replaced by a firecracker or popper. The lights on the minarets of a mosque are also lit. Perhaps the most widely watched sign in modern Turkey is the television: the *iftar* is on TV. Ticker tape at the bottom of the screen shows the exact time of *iftar* for each town. During the hour leading up to and after the breaking of the fast, television programs focus on religious subjects—pictures of mosques, Islamic music, debates between Muslim scholars, and Koran chanting.

Keeping the fast is hard in hot weather. It is hardest for cigarette smokers! Just before *iftar*, bad tempers can explode and traffic jams increase as everyone rushes to where they'll be eating *iftar*. More traffic accidents occur at this time. Don't try to get a taxi—they will not be interested in picking up a passenger. Also, don't expect someone to do heavy physical work for a prolonged period (workmen and maids go slower during Ramadan).

The *iftar* is a huge meal. Sometimes people eat more during Ramadan than normal, and gain weight. You may expect there to be little interest in food during a month of fasting, but the reverse is true. Women take great pride in preparing their best cuisine for the *iftar*; magazines are full of recipe ideas, and afternoon TV shows have celebrity chefs hosting cooking programs.

Businesses and organizations may host an *iftar* meal at a hotel or restaurant for important contacts. It is an honor to be invited, and one should never refuse. Ramadan is also an important time for almsgiving. Local authorities will erect a Ramadan tent in the center of town providing a free *iftar* meal for the needy. This can also be supported by contributions from wealthy donors.

There are Ramadan traditions: in the days of the sultans, it was a festival time. Dishes usually not seen at the rest of the year are served—Ramadan *pide*, a special bread, is delicious, and lines of fasters can form outside bakeries before *iftar*. In the evening during Ramadan more men are likely to go to the mosque, and local authorities may put on traditional

entertainment such as jugglers, firecrackers, and puppet shows.

Surprisingly enough, not all Turks participate in the fast. Restaurants and cafés in big cities are open. It is considerate not to eat in the street, however. You may be offered water or tea in business meetings or in a shop during Ramadan. It is not offensive to accept, even if some present are fasting; it is seen as being of extra value to fast when someone else is drinking. If you ask someone whether they are fasting or not, one who is fasting will say "*niyetliyim*," which means "I intend" (to complete the fast). The correct reply to this is "*Allah kabul etsin*"—"May God accept it."

Ramadan Holiday (*Şeker Bayramı: Eid al-Fitr*)
This is a three-day feast to celebrate the end of the month of Ramadan. The Turkish name means "sugar holiday." Everyone buys candy to give as presents or to hand out to children who knock on their door. The first day is reserved for family celebrations. The whole family gathers at the home of the oldest person to show respect and kiss the elder's hand. The children receive *Bayram harç* (pocket money) from the older relatives. It is usual for the whole family to visit the graves of

departed older relatives,
and to pray for their souls.

Friends and family spend
the next two days visiting
with candies. In offices,
chocolates are given to
employees and business contacts.

Kandil

Kandil days are commemorative days that are not
holidays from work. These days of particular
religious significance are Muhammad's birthday,
the night of Muhammad's conception (believed
to be a time to receive forgiveness and mercy),
the Night of Forgiveness, the Night of Power
and Destiny (the night the Koran was given to
Muhammad), and the night of the Night Journey
(when Muhammad visited heaven). Minarets are
lit up for these occasions. A special ring pastry
called *Kandil simidi* is made. The television will
show religious programs: a sermon and a reading
from the Koran, often transmitted from a mosque.

Devout Muslims may hold a religious ceremony
(*mevlut*) at home. An *imam* (prayer leader), or,
among certain sects, the *dede* (spiritual leader),
both of whom can be called *hoca* (teacher), will
lead chanting of the Koran and recite religious
poems. Women wear headscarves and dress
modestly. If you are present, remember that at
one point the worshipers will turn to face Mecca.
There is a closing prayer and the guests' hands are
sprinkled with rosewater. After the ceremony the
host offers refreshments.

Other Religious Festivals

Other religious festivals are celebrated on a local basis around Turkey. For example, an Alevi holiday is held in the town of Hacıbektaş every August. This is a three-day celebration, attended by many Alevi Muslims, who camp in the area. It celebrates the teaching of Hacıbektaş, the founder of an important Dervish order in the twelfth century. The most famous saying of his is "Be master of your hand, your loins, and your tongue."

The Mevlana festival is held every December in Konya, where Dervishes dance in accordance with the teachings of the great mystic poet of Islam, Mevlana, also known as Rumi (1207–73). They wear white robes and conical hats, and twirl to drums and a shepherd's pipe. The mesmerizing circular dance represents the harmony of the

spheres and is an expression of cosmic love. It lasts for about an hour. The dancers hold one hand up to God and one hand down to the earth, symbolizing union with God through trance. This Sufi dance was banned under Atatürk. Recently, it has been revived as part of Turkey's social history.

Another significant annual religious event is the Hajj to Mecca. Pilgrims are often the elderly. In smaller towns, it is common to have a big celebration to send people off and welcome them back. During the time of Hajj, the bus terminals and airports are packed with pilgrims wearing the simple white robe. Those returning are called *hacı*—one who has done the Hajj. *Hacıs* have the right to paint the gates of their garden or building entrance green. When someone has made the Hajj, it is good to visit the *hacı*, and in return you will receive a present such as prayer beads or water from the holy well in Mecca.

Aşure **Time**
This is a special time in the year when women prepare *aşure* pudding and give it to their neighbors. *Aşure* is known as Noah's pudding, and it is a sweet dessert cooked using all the grains and fruits that Noah was assumed to have taken into the ark.

REGIONAL FESTIVALS
Regions have annual festivals, often linked with sport or with local agricultural produce, such as:
January: Selçuk (camel wrestling)

May: Silifke (music and folklore), Tekirdağ (cherry festival)
June: Bursa (silk festival)
July: Edirne (traditional grease wrestling), Akşehir Nasreddin Hoca festival
October: Antalya (international arts festival)
December: Demre festival (Saint Nicholas), Konya Mevlana festival

TURKISH TRADITIONS

As we have seen, to be a Turk is to be a Muslim.
Secular Turks will still call themselves Muslim, even
though they do not attend the mosque regularly
and do not uphold the five pillars of Islam. They
participate in many of the customs, such as
circumcision, and will join in some of the fast and
special meals during Ramadan. This is done partly
out of social solidarity. Religious festivals and
beliefs give a structure and a unity to social life,
which is deeply valued by Turks.

Turkey is a country of diversity. There are the
modernists/secularists who want to travel, shop,
learn about other cultures, and try new ideas.
Then there are others who want to appear very
traditional and pious. The women wear
headscarves and the men have beards and carry
prayer beads. There are thirty-three beads on a
strand; by thumbing through it three times, one has
recited the ninety-nine names of Allah. In practice,
many men just fiddle with their beads, using them
as worry beads. This is an example of a custom
that is not directly in line with orthodox Muslim
teaching but is derived from cultural practice.
There are many similar examples in Turkish
culture, some of which are fusions of Islam with
the shamanism or folk religion of the Turks'
nomadic ancestors.

Folklore and Superstition

Depending on economic and religious status,
individuals can be quite superstitious. The evil
eye is considered to be the main cause of many

misfortunes, and it is seen everywhere, with the blue and white bead used to protect against it. Blue eyes are believed to be a natural protection against the evil eye. If you have blue eyes, people may stare at them because they are uncommon.

A *cin*, pronounced "jinn," is believed by Muslims to be a living spirit or genie. These are always present around humans, but unseen. There are both good and evil jinns, who can cause sickness, insanity, or death. The majority of Turks fear them and take them seriously. A common belief is that it is wrong to compliment a baby. Turks purposely say a baby is ugly, or call it *Satılmış* ("sold") so the jinn will not want to steal it away or send it an illness. It is also believed that excessive praise may draw an evil jinn's attention to someone good, and cause the jinn to hurt the person out of jealousy. The word "*Maşallah*" is used to ward off the evil eye and is often said after giving praise.

People often pray at saints' tombs for a good outcome. Different tombs are believed to be effective for different requests, such as good crops, conceiving, receiving healing, or finding a marriage partner. Normally when a Turk visits the tomb he makes a vow and a bargain with God. If his prayer comes true he will do some righteous deed. You'll notice that at a holy place, such as a shrine or tomb, Turks tie a string or a strip of cloth on a sacred tree to make a wish.

When out and about, you will see advertised in café windows: "We read coffee grounds." Turks are interested in all aspects of fortune-telling, by astrologers or gypsies, studying coffee grounds, or using rabbits. On the street you may see a man with a rabbit. You pay him for the rabbit to choose you a slip of paper, which tells your fortune.

Turks make a "tsk tsk" noise and/or pull an earlobe while knocking on a table for luck. Knocking on a table is a superstition similar to "knock on wood," and will usually follow a positive statement or wish about the future. Words such as "*inşallah*" ("God willing") are used to avoid tempting fate.

Curses are feared by many Turks. Even the beggar on the street may put a curse on a passerby who does not give him anything. Since Turks can hold a grudge for life, they may arrange for a curse to be put on a person with whom they are upset. A *hoca* is a Muslim shaman skilled in these things. He can also break a curse that someone is believed to have put on you.

The Koran is placed on a high shelf in the home and is thought of as an amulet against evil—for example, it is believed that a soldier carrying the Koran will not be shot in battle. Women sew paper inscribed with verses of the Koran into the folds of a sick person's clothes for healing. A Turk will recite the *Bismillah*, the first verse of the Koran, at the beginning of a journey, when scared, or at night before going to bed to ward off evil: "In the name of Allah, the most merciful, the most compassionate." The *Bismillah* is often hung in homes, shops, offices, and restaurants.

For a blessing, an animal will sometimes be sacrificed at the start of something new, such as the foundation of a new building or opening of a new workplace.

Dreams are thought to be very significant in foretelling the future. Some people are considered gifted in interpretation. Usually if a dream foretells something good and comes true, the person who benefited will give a small gift to the person who had the dream. It is not unusual for a friend to say, "I saw you in my dream last night," and attach importance to this.

The concept of *kismet* has a major role in individuals' lives. This is a belief in fate and in the predetermination of events, described by Turks as the "command of God"—a belief that one's personal needs, friendships, marriage, disasters, and accidents are all predestined. This mindset can sometimes lead Turks to be weak in the areas of taking control of life and future planning. It also leads them to be accepting of their lot.

Two contrasting proverbs shed light on the degree of fatalism in different sections of Turkish society. One reads "I found food today, I'll eat today: Tomorrow? Ah well, God is great." This reflects a belief that all our accomplishments are only possible through the grace of Allah. The second teaches "First tie your camel to the tree, then pray to God for its protection"—that is, while ultimately the blessing comes from Allah, he expects you to play your part in making it happen.

chapter four

MAKING FRIENDS

WORK AND SOCIAL LIFE

Turks like to do things in groups, not individually or in pairs; they believe "the more the merrier." They are hospitable and will treat you as one of the family, particularly if you are staying alone in a hotel room or rented business apartment. They tend not to understand if you want to be independent; they are afraid that you will be lonely, and will make a serious effort to look after you. This immediate warmth and generosity should not be confused with real friendship, however, which will only develop over time.

Real friendship implies a commitment to and concern for the other person. Turks expect to see their friends often and to be intimately concerned with their lives. It is important to contact friends regularly, and foreigners who don't do this are generally thought "cold."

Privacy is not generally understood. Someone who has been ill would expect you to want all the details of their doctor's visit, and if you didn't ask would assume you didn't care. Turks use flowery language, so it is important to use phrases such as "I've missed you a lot."

The Turks are extremely proud of their nation, its past and, in the case of secular Turks, Atatürk's reforms. They will want to take you to historical sites and also to modern facilities to show you that Turkey has all the amenities available in Europe. The visitor needs to be careful in making comparisons because they are sensitive to criticism. If you remember the Turkish worldview, its core values of shame, honor, loyalty, and unity, you will recognize the patterns of deeper meaning behind your hosts' behavior.

Phrase Your Questions with Care!

Turks don't want to disappoint you. An experienced shopper in an Istanbul market would not ask, "These peppers aren't hot and spicy, are they?" Such a question is guaranteed to get the answer "no," as the shopper has expressed a clear preference. It is far safer to ask "Are these spicy or not?" in a way that prevents the vendor from guessing the answer you want!

Turkish people often feel personally responsible for the success of a visitor's stay. They do not want you to be disappointed and may plan a series of outings for you. If they feel that you are not enjoying yourself they may redouble their efforts to ensure that you have a good experience.

GREETINGS

Introductions and greetings are very important. There are set patterns. Generally people greet each other with a kiss on both cheeks, man to man or woman to woman. This is common in a business context, too, if there is a long-standing relationship between the two parties. An appropriate greeting from man to woman is either a nod or a "dead fish" handshake with as little contact as possible if you do not know each other well. Sometimes, as a sign of respect for the elderly, younger people may kiss the hand and press it to their forehead.

When you are introduced to someone for the first time, you should reply "*Memnun oldum*" ("Pleased to meet you"). When entering someone's home, or a meeting room, or joining a restaurant table full of people, it is important to go around and greet everyone present, not just the people you know, and perhaps shake the hand of each person. If an elderly person or a more senior business associate enters after you, it is polite to stand up for him or her. The greeting itself is important, and certain key phrases need to be learned. As you enter, individuals will say "*Hoş geldiniz!*" ("Welcome!"). You should reply "*Hoş bulduk!*"

("Glad to be here!"). As with most areas of life in modern Turkey, religious and secular people behave differently. Your religious friend is more likely to greet you with "*Selam aleyküm*" ("May God's peace be with you"); the reply to this is "*Aleyküm selam*" ("And also with you").

ATTITUDES TOWARD FOREIGNERS

Turkish people are courteous to strangers. They are hospitable people. Turks have an expression about visitors: "*Tanrı misafiri*" ("God's guest"—a visitor must be looked after as if he had been sent to you as an envoy from God). Other Turkish proverbs that reflect this attitude are "A guest comes with ten blessings, eats one and leaves nine," and "The master of the house is the servant of the guest." The foreigner who is the guest of a Turk will experience royal treatment.

The wealthier sections of Turkish society will have traveled, and may even have lived abroad for education or work. The rest of the nation forms their view of foreigners through Hollywood films, foreign serials shown on Turkish TV, and meeting tourists. This gives them a selective view of what life is like abroad, and what foreigners are like. Many less well-educated lower-class Turks have the impression that the streets of Europe and America are paved with gold, and want to emigrate. They may find it hard to understand why one who has a sought-after foreign passport might wish to make the opposite journey.

While Turks believe, in general, that life abroad may be better than in Turkey, national pride means that they will not readily admit to this. In general, Europeans and Americans are considered to be well-educated, to have good business ethics, and to be strong in areas such as planning ahead. However, they are also considered to display negative qualities such as individualism and competitiveness, and to be distant or cold.

In business, many Turkish companies are eager to work in partnership with foreign firms as foreigners are seen as bringing know-how, in the form of either management practice or specialist knowledge. The Turkish partner would bring expertise in distribution, would be familiar with the regulations, and would have a network of local contacts. Some of the most successful companies in Turkey are such joint ventures.

However, some ultra-nationalists believe that there should be no need for foreign goods or foreign-run companies in Turkey. When a problem arises often the blame will be shifted on to "foreign provocation."

JOINING CLUBS

There are many clubs and associations that businesspeople can join. International clubs represented in Turkey and run by Turks include the Rotary Club and the Lion's Club, both of which are very active in charitable work. Associations exist in most of the big cities that function as support and social networks for foreigners resident in Turkey, such as the American Women's Association and International Women of Istanbul. The embassies in

Ankara and consulates in Istanbul are also hubs of social life for the communities of their own nationals.

Sports and general interest clubs do exist, but are not widespread. You can become a member of a sports center or gym in the large cities. Golf courses and country clubs are less common and more exclusive. Soccer and basketball teams are fairly common but other sports can be difficult to find, as can amateur music and drama societies.

INVITATIONS HOME

Turks are wonderful hosts. When invited, always accept—it is rude not to. The foreign visitor may be surprised at various customs, and concerned about making a social faux pas. Watch what the others do, and do the same. If they take their shoes off at the door, you should too. Slippers will be provided. A little refreshing cologne will be poured into your cupped hands. Wipe your hands together and rub the back of your neck with it.

Two or three generations may live under one roof, which can be daunting when you are first introduced, but remember to greet everyone in the room. If you are sitting down when new guests arrive, stand up to greet them.

The Turkish hostess will ensure that everyone is comfortable. An evening meal may start late; the usual time is about 8:00 p.m. You are not expected to arrive exactly at the mealtime—usually you will be invited earlier, so that you can sit and talk with your hosts first. Wait to be invited to the table.

During the meal, your hostess will want to look after you and will offer to serve you each dish. Don't serve yourself. A lovely Turkish custom is to say the phrase "*Afiyet olsun!*" ("*Bon appetit*") to each other at the table. There is a special phrase to say to the cook—it is "*Elinize sağlık*" ("Health to your hands"). When you have eaten everything on your plate, your hostess will offer you more. It is important for Turkish hosts to be sure that they have done their best for you in serving you a large and wonderful meal, so even if you refuse, she may press you several times to have an extra helping. If you are full you can refuse, complimenting her on the food; placing your right hand palm down on your chest is a polite way of both expressing gratitude for the food and showing that you are full and do not want more. Depending on the situation, the hostess may not sit at the table, but just serve all the time. If your hosts have children, don't be surprised at how late they stay up.

When dinner is over, even though it may seem late, you should not leave right away. Enjoying the company after the meal is important. Then, when the evening seems to have come to an end, don't just get up and say you have to go. Start the process gently by dropping a few hints that you will need to leave soon. You are asking permission to leave. A short time later you should mention it again. Your host will try to encourage you to stay longer. When you are preparing to leave, they will insist on helping you with your coat. Your shoes should be put on in the hallway by the door or outside the door in the building.

As a guest you are entitled to respect. You are in a special category and will be treated and served well. Your host will expect to put on a spread (if not, they will feel they have been rude)—a potluck supper is definitely not Turkish! Even if you're dropping in for coffee your host will produce a range of both sweet and savory food to accompany it. The visitor should realize that if an offer is extended to stop by any time, it is truly meant and taken literally. Your Turkish friend will be offended if you wait for an invitation for a definite time. Conversely, your Turkish friend may call on you when you least expect it.

GIFT GIVING

When visiting someone in their home, take a small gift such as flowers or chocolate. The gift should always be wrapped, in wrapping paper or even in a plastic bag. It should not normally be handed to the host; just place it in the hallway or on a table. Your hostess will probably not open it in front of you. If a gift needs to be handed to the recipient (for example, in the case of a birthday), this should be done without a lot of attention.

Be careful not to compliment your host on something or it may be given to you as a gift. Appreciating a picture or vase or other possession may be taken as a request for it to be given to you.

It is quite usual for people in an apartment complex to offer some cooking to their neighbors if they have had a baking day. Also, you may be given food to welcome you to the apartment when you move in. If your neighbor gives you a plate of food you should accept it, but don't return the plate empty. Fill it with some food of your own.

MANNERS

In social settings, age is respected. Turks will show deference to an older person by giving them the most comfortable seat, allowing them to choose the music or TV program, and listening to their opinions without disagreeing.

It is considered extremely rude in Turkey to interrupt someone who is speaking, even if they are wrong. Listening is a sign of respect. Looking bored, looking away or at paperwork, or checking your watch is rude—not only does it show disrespect but it dishonors the speaker in front of all the others present. One should look attentive.

However strange you may find some of these customs, be respectful, and remember that the way people look at the universe is affected by their upbringing and deeply ingrained values. Sometimes it may be wiser not to give your opinion but just to nod to indicate that you are listening. Even though things may not be what you are used to, it is impolite to criticize Turkey, your elders, or your hosts. If you have a different opinion, or disagree in a social context, it is best to say nothing. Don't take it upon yourself to be the one to correct an accepted historical view. Certain political issues, such as Kurds and Armenians, should be avoided.

chapter five

PRIVATE & FAMILY LIFE

CHANGING SOCIAL STRUCTURE

Turkish social structure is a fusion of the Ottoman Empire's Islamic values and the modern Republic's secular values. For the most part a mutual synthesis of these two different, even antagonistic, cultures has been achieved. Only relatively recently has Turkey become more polarized, and cultural differences and clashes can be seen.

The population movement from rural to urban areas over the past half-century has been significant, bringing about major changes in the family structure. Family still plays an central role, however.

THE FAMILY

The importance of the family can be seen in the fact that Turkish has a special vocabulary for family relationships. Thus, specific words indicate whether a person belongs to the husband's or the wife's side of the family, or is an older or younger sibling.

Generally speaking, especially among poorer, less educated, or religious people, men will be honored before women. A sister will defer to a brother, even if he is younger. There are certain societal expectations. Family members have to look after the weak and elderly. A household normally consists of a married couple and their children, and may well include elderly parents and unmarried brothers or sisters.

Regardless of where family members live, they all have particular responsibilities and together serve the common good of the family. This includes physical protection, economic support, and upholding the reputation of the family.

Individualism is not encouraged in Turkey. The group concept is strong. You have a responsibility to others in the group; a Turkish proverb reads, "Look after the orphan, feed the hungry, separate the fighters in a quarrel." Along with this comes an emphasis on the group view. People do not want to make decisions on an individual basis, even on the smallest thing. Ask a group of Turks what they would like to eat and most will hesitate to make suggestions. They each want to say what they think the others would want to hear. Turks are open to new ideas as long as those ideas do not interfere with group solidarity.

LIVING CONDITIONS

Most housing in Turkey, especially in urban areas, consists of apartment complexes. More recently, a number of gated communities have been built and are popular. Often extended families purchase separate apartments in the same building. A large percentage of the population will rent their apartment. In the towns and villages small houses are gradually being knocked down and apartment complexes built in their place. In Turkey the concept

of farming is different from America and Europe. Rather than living in isolated farmhouses, Turkish farmers live in the village and commute daily to the fields to work.

Much importance is placed on making a good impression on visitors. Wherever you visit in Turkey, a formal room is always kept very clean and tidy for entertaining guests, with furnishings covered when not in use. There is usually a second room for use by the family.

Balconies are important, particularly in the summer. They serve as a place for entertainment and relaxation. In long summer evenings the family may eat on the balcony and sit talking and relaxing in the night air. A more recent trend in new buildings is to not have open balconies. Part of this is due to the availablility of air-conditioning and white goods.

In general, there is a strong sense of neighborliness. Turks often welcome newcomers to the building. Housewives will often meet during the day for tea parties, rotating from house to house

each week. Apartment buildings usually have a
janitor, or *kapıcı*, who acts as caretaker and does
small jobs for the tenants such as daily shopping for
newspapers and bread and taking out the trash. He
often has a small living quarter in the basement for
his family and may receive some salary, covered by
a monthly service charge paid by each apartment.

Furnishings and Appliances
In villages furnishing can be very basic, consisting
of a carpet, couch and/or cushions to sit on around
the wall. The room will have a large cupboard and
china cabinet for storage. Every house will have a TV
set. In the city, the style will be Western. The formal
living room will have a fashionable suite and wall-
to-wall carpets or lovely rugs. Since the early 1980s
the Turkish market has been flooded with electrical
appliances. The very latest designs, as well as pirated
copies, are available. Most homes will have a TV,
DVD player, stereo system, refrigerator, dishwasher,
microwave, washing machine, and so on.

DAILY LIFE AND ROUTINE

Turkish society is undergoing a radical transformation. There has been considerable progress toward raising the status of women in terms of autonomy and rights, and women are achieving greater independence through higher levels of education and employment.

Traditionally, in daily life men deal with the world outside the family. They are the protectors and women submit to their authority. The woman's role is to care for the family. In a rural setting, a woman's world is her children, household, and pride in domestic skills. In urban areas and among the middle and upper classes, however, women may be more active in the public realm. The cost of living in the large cities, particularly if families want to provide their children with private education and other opportunities, means that more Turkish women are going out to work. This broadens their horizons, gives them a sense of financial independence, and changes their expectations.

Professional or career women take pride in both their home and their work. Educated middle-class women have more say in decision making, choice of spouse, and size of family, and more economic independence and involvement in public life. In general women who exhibit maturity and wisdom are respected in the public sector.

Modern Turks jokingly describe these roles as "Minister of State" and "Minister of Foreign Affairs." The wife will run the home, the man the external life of the family. A Turkish man does not generally help around the house.

The honor of the family is reflected in its outward appearance; home and public areas are kept clean. Windows are ritually washed at least once a week, sometimes every day. Cleaning and cooking are important for Turkish women.

Modern Turkish women may do their weekly shopping at the supermarket, but they will make a point of going to the weekly bazaar to buy fresh fruit and vegetables. These bazaars are set up in different

areas of the city on different days, and a number of residential roads are closed for the bazaar stalls and awnings to be set up. For daily needs, on nearly every corner there is a mini-supermarket or a small grocer called a *bakkal*. These are usually open until 9:00 or 10:00 p.m. If you live in a building with a grocer on the ground floor, there is a unique system of lowering a basket on a long rope from the window, with a note in it listing your needs. The grocer puts the items in the basket and you pull the basket up. Shopping done!

Urban Life
Turkey's cities are sophisticated, middle-class centers with full amenities. In the last two decades, due mainly to industrialization, the Turkish population has changed significantly from being rural to urban. This has had deep socioeconomic and cultural repercussions. Turkey's cities have experienced sweeping demographic changes and developmental challenges.

The metropolitan centers are encircled by slum dwellings called *gecekondu*, which means "built during the night." These slums were originally created by newly arrived migrants, many of whom have now lived in them for years. When visitors see these areas they comment on how unfinished they look. The migrants arrive and build four simple walls with a roof. As money becomes available another floor is added and more relatives from the village can come to live. Gradually the local authorities connect gas, electricity, and water services to these areas, and build roads.

Rural Life

Village life is hard, and poverty is widespread. It is a world controlled by men, where much of the hard labor both in and out of the home is done by women. It is also typically feudal. The landowners control the villages and regions, and many of the farms are owned by one wealthy man who hires the workers. Turkey is fairly self-sufficient; it produces its own food supply and exports to neighboring countries. While the rural areas are poor and their production lacks technology, they have real potential for agricultural development and growth, hindered mainly by mismanagement and fear of upsetting the powerful rural elite.

Rural families tend to have many children. Education is not a high priority, particularly for girls. Often when young people come of age they move to an urban area. As a result, the villages are more conservative and superstitious. Each is a closely knit society. Villagers are generously hospitable to outsiders who do not threaten their customs. Generally, they do not like photographs of women to be taken. If visiting villagers it is best to go in the late afternoon or early evening, when work in the field has been completed. Because of transportation schedules it may be necessary to stay overnight—the host will urge the visitor to stay longer. It is the guest's choice to stay as long as he wants, and a good host will not ask, "How long are you staying?"

Children

Turks love children. Adults pinch the cheeks of a pretty child to let them know that they are loved.

People stop to watch a child go by, and even macho teenage boys will fuss over a baby.

Children are not held to a strict routine. They stay up late and get taken everywhere. The idea of a babysitter to enable mom and dad to go out alone is foreign. Turks love to take their children with them. Children are welcome everywhere, even in smart restaurants and hotels, and they are not much reprimanded—it is believed that children should not be disciplined for what they cannot understand. Even older children are unlikely to be disciplined in public. Older ones help with their younger siblings. Often the *abla* (eldest sister) is eager to be given special responsibility to help with the younger children.

In modern Turkish cities, it is expensive to raise children; the trend for middle-class families who wish to give their children a private education and other advantages is to have just one child or to have a fairly large age gap

between children. However, in order to stop the population from falling, Prime Minister Erdoğan has publicly, and somewhat controversially, encouraged families to have at least three children.

Changing Lifestyles

Turkey has become a consumer society, and this has been accompanied by rising expectations. Over the past decade it has enjoyed an economic boom that has benefited not ony the secular urban elites, but also the conservative supporters of the AKP governing party and former rural entrepreneurs. Their unprecedented upward mobility has led to the formation of an Islamic, urban middle class.

This new Islamic bourgeoisie has money to spend, and the opportunities to do so are increasingly diverse: luxury gated communities, restaurants and hotels catering to a more pious lifestyle are springing up in urban centers.

Modernization and industrialization have resulted in a shift away from Turkey's traditional, male-dominated society to consumer-led egalitarianism. Twenty or thirty years ago it was rare to see women in certain parts of town buying electrical goods, as these were male preserves. Today such goods are available in large, brightly lit shopping malls. And there are now vast, multinational supermarkets in the big cities that are packed with shoppers in the evenings and on weekends.

Lifestyle differences vary with the level of industrialization. Family authority patterns are being affected. Greater educational opportunities mean that younger members of a family may quite easily earn more than their parents. Also, Turks now in their thirties and forties grew up at a time when there were many shortages. They want their own children to have all the opportunities they missed; this often results in children being materialistically focused. A shift in the rights of the individual is in progress, with a growing emphasis on personal desires and abilities, freedom to make decisions for oneself, equality of the sexes, and a more egalitarian power structure. Now that some women work outside the home, children may go to nurseries or kindergartens. In the cities, family units may be smaller, as young couples become more mobile and live further away from their relatives. Because of this, fewer relatives may live in the same building, and as strangers move in Turks may complain that there is less neighborliness than there used to be.

Fashion
People in urban areas are very fashion-conscious. Turks always look stylish when they go out and when they receive guests. It is part of one's honor and self-respect to be well-dressed. Importance is placed on designer labels and having fashionable clothes. A large part of a working woman's salary is spent on clothing and cosmetics. It would be shameful for her to go out not looking her best.

Clean shoes matter. Shoes should be kept polished and shining. If you have walked in a muddy street, wipe your shoes with a cloth before entering a building. When wearing sandals, toenails should be neat and clean. Turkish women love to have manicures and pedicures.

Turks are becoming more aware of the importance of good health and being in shape. Gyms and beauty salons are springing up in the wealthier parts of cities. If you can't get away from the office for a vacation, you go to the solarium for a tan. If you have to wear glasses they should be an expensive make, but it is better still to have laser treatment to give you perfect vision.

Even conservative Muslim women are fashion-conscious. There are "rules" governing the make, design, and tying of your headscarf, and many women are wearing designer jeans under their long raincoats and robes. Within different parameters, their fashion sense finds expression

FAMILY OCCASIONS
Births
Turks, we have seen, are very family-oriented. Although birthrate statistics are high, modern urbanites increasingly choose to have only one or two children, and to give birth at a hospital. Private hospitals offer the most modern technology, advice, and good prenatal care. These women tend to prefer a caesarean birth. Rural women tend to give birth at home with a midwife.

Village tradition is for grandparents to choose the baby's name. Urban Turks choose their child's name, but may keep with tradition by having another name given by elderly relatives. Turks use the second of two names; for example, Mehmet Cenk Atakan would be known as Cenk Atakan or M. Cenk Atakan (Cenk may be chosen by the parents, Mehmet by an elderly relative). There may be a religious ceremony for naming the baby, involving an *imam* coming to the home and reciting from the Koran. The *imam* then whispers into the baby's ear, "Your name is . . ." The ceremony ends with a blessing on the household.

In urban areas children of either sex are valued, although sons are preferred. In villages a son is more valuable because he brings growth to the family through marriage, whereas the daughter will grow up, marry, and leave it. (If there is a lull in conversation and everyone falls silent, someone may say "A daughter has been born"—that is, something has happened to put a damper on the party!) A family member may shoot a rifle into the air to celebrate the birth.

The child is registered as belonging to the extended family of the parents. The registration involves much detail: each family has a number. This is representative of the wider clan, not the small family unit, and the child will be allocated an ordinal number showing its position in the clan (number one was the oldest person back in the Atatürk era). Before the end of the twentieth century birth dates may have been recorded incorrectly, particularly in rural areas.

It is usual for friends and family to visit the mother and baby as soon as possible after the birth, and bring gifts for the baby. Turks tend not to buy much before the birth, for fear of tempting fate. It is customary for the mother and baby not to go out for the first forty days.

Circumcision

Circumcision is a rite of passage for a boy. It signifies his becoming a man. This practice derives from the Hadith traditions and is one of the signs of being a Muslim. Usually the son is circumcised around the age of eight, but some families may have two sons circumcised at the same time because of the expense of separate parties. The circumcision party involves the boy wearing a special suit for a week before, just like a little sultan with his sequined cape, hat, and scepter.

A popular custom is to parade the child around town in a convoy of cars, with much honking of horns. Religious families have a recital of a poem about Muhammad just before the circumcision. The actual ceremony is usually performed in public on a white bed. The child receives a lot of presents—often toy guns and the like. A wealthy businessman may show his benevolence by paying for the requisite party for poor boys in the neighborhood, or for the sons of his employees.

National Service

The phrase *"En büyük asker bizim asker"*—"The greatest soldier is our soldier"—is very popular. After age eighteen, every man has to do eighteen months of paid military service, or he can choose to do fewer months and receive no salary. Every so often the government offers the option of paying a large sum and doing just one month. Over the last few decades, problems in the southeast have discouraged individuals from signing up for fear of being sent there as part of their service.

When a young man leaves for military service, his friends give him a big send-off. This moment is another significant rite of passage. All enlistees have one month of training, and assignments are then made based on education and skill level. The better educated get office jobs and other strategic appointments. The army reinforces national unity and promotes the strong secular teaching that upholds the Republic. Also, it often helps village youths to improve their reading and social skills.

As in many countries, when older men get together to drink they tell national service stories. Every Turkish male is theoretically part of the army reserve and can be called up in a time of war.

Marriage
Young people mostly go out in a group; couples tend not to go out in public without a chaperon. Spending time alone together is seen as extremely loose, and endangers the girl's reputation.

Marriage generally involves the family and its approval to some degree. Arranged marriages still take place in villages, or among the very wealthy, where there may be an alliance of interests. Among more conservative people, family members have a say in the choice of partner. Often the groom will be considerably older than the bride because he has completed military service and has had to work to earn some money before considering marriage. Marrying for love is becoming common among young middle-class urban Turks, and they sometimes do so without parental consent.

The bride and her family will have been preparing a *çeyiz* (dowry), which includes clothing and household goods. This is kept for the daughter until a marriage date has been set. When a couple decides to get married there are certain steps to be taken: *sözlü*, *nişanlı*, and *evli*.

Sözlü is a pre-engagement arrangement. This officially sanctions the couple seeing each other and spending time together, although not alone. It is a serious commitment, and it is considered a grave breach of honor to break it.

Nişanlı means "engaged." The process of becoming engaged involves all members of both families. The hopeful bridegroom's family goes to the woman's family to ask for her hand in marriage. This is a formal visit; they will be wearing their best clothes and will be given the best refreshments. In order for the man not to lose face, his prospective bride answers his proposal in a subtle way. She makes coffee, and if she wishes to accept the proposal (or is instructed to do so by her mother) she puts sugar in his cup. If she rejects it, she puts salt in the cup.

A party is given to celebrate the engagement, overseen by the family elder. In a ceremony two rings tied to the ends of a ribbon are presented to the groom- and bride-to-be: each puts a ring on their finger and the elder cuts the ribbon.

Evli means "married." The first part of the marriage celebration is the *kına gecesi* (henna party). This is a party given for the bride by a few close friends, a married sister, or the older female relatives. It is a major event in the village. At a certain stage in the evening the single girls will walk in a circle around the bride, carrying candles and handkerchiefs containing henna. The bride is then encouraged to open her hand by the mother-in-law offering her a coin. She and her friends will place the henna on their hands. They dance and sing sad songs about losing their friend to another village. Married friends will tell all sorts of horror stories about mothers-in-law.

The official wedding ceremony is civil. The couple obtains a license to marry from the local authority, and an official conducts the ceremony, which is relatively short. If held in a registry office, it is a little like a conveyor belt, so wealthy families prefer to pay to perform the ceremony at home or in a hotel. A religious wedding is possible, but it is a criminal offense to conduct it before the civil ceremony. It is also an offense to have more than one wife.

During the ceremony, right from the moment when the bride and groom come in, there is a lot of applause. People applaud when "yes" is said and upon the announcement that the couple are married. The bride and groom also try to step on each other's feet. It is believed this will show who will rule the house during the marriage!

Large bouquets of flowers are sent, many photographs are taken, and videos are made. It is customary to give money, gold, and bracelets. The

lower classes make a large demonstration of this.
Those giving money pin it on to the bride's dress or
the groom's collar.

There is a wedding party afterward. This varies
in degree according to circumstances. Every guest
is given a little souvenir—a piece of candy, such as
a sugarcoated almond, or a small present.

After the couple is married, they need to get a
family identity card. The bride is removed from the
register of her old family and added to that of her
husband. Usually new couples move into fully
furnished apartments. Traditionally, their parents
are allotted certain rooms to furnish in full.

Dealing with Illness

In traditional Turkish culture, health is considered
to be a blessing from God. It is always polite to ask
about the health of other people and their family.
Turks may believe that an illness is a result of God's
punishment, retribution for doing wrong, worry,
being the victim of maliciously intended magic, or
offending or harming a jinn (evil spirit), in
addition to the usual medical explanations.

Sickness is dealt with in many ways. A proverb
from eastern Turkey says "When God gave a
problem he also gave the remedy." Traditional as well
as Western medical treatment may be used. Turkish
hospitals and medical practitioners are as good as
any in Europe, yet most housewives have their own
set of recommended cures. Yogurt is considered
good for stomach problems. Tying a scarf tightly
around one's forehead helps with headaches.
Midwives are particularly popular in the villages;

these are older, experienced women who have
knowledge of traditional methods of healing. For
those who are more superstitious there are other
people who are believed to have special healing
powers. Muslim religious leaders can cure by
making an amulet or armband bearing verses
from the Koran.

The shrines of certain saints are known to have
healing powers. People will travel great distances to
visit a shrine or special spa where it is believed the
place or the water may cure their ills.

Funerals
Death is generally considered to be the will of God.
This does not mean that grief and emotion are at all
lessened. When people refer to a deceased person
they will often add the adjective *rahmetli* (with the
mercy of God) to the person's name.

A visit to the deceased's family is appropriate.
Turks will drop everything to run to the side of
friends or family who have suffered a loss. There are
certain phrases that it is polite to say to the bereaved,
such as *"Baş ınız sağolsun"* ("Health to your head"),
"Allah rahmet eylesin" ("May God grant them
mercy"), and *"Allah sabır versin"* ("May God give
you patience").

The body should be buried within twenty-four
hours. At the service the *Fatiha*, the first chapter of
the Koran, is recited. Praise is offered to Allah, and
then a petition for his mercy on the souls of all
present and on the soul of the deceased. Then
follows the most important communal act: the
discharge. The *imam* asks "What was the deceased

person like to you?" The reply is "We found him/her to be a good person." The *imam* asks "Do you forgive them anything they have done?" The reply is "We forgive them." This is your "final duty" to the deceased, and it is very important to attend the funeral and give them this absolution.

The crowd carries the coffin to the hearse. Burials are in municipal cemeteries, which are planted with cypress trees. The body is buried intact as Muslims believe in bodily resurrection at judgment day. It is taken out of the coffin and buried in its shroud.

The last respectful act is a prayer: "O servant of God, say that my god is Allah, and my prophet is Muhammad and my book is the Koran and my religion is Islam."

Rather than sending wreaths and flowers, in Turkey donations are made to charity. At the mosque different charities have stands for donations, or a gift may be sent directly to the charity in memory of the deceased.

It is customary to have a religious ceremony seven days after death and again forty days later, in which the Koran will be read in the home. It is also tradition to distribute a piece of *lokma*, a sweet pastry, at the end of the ceremony. This is done in memory of the deceased. The family will regularly go to the graveside to pray; the deceased are to be visited, greeted, and remembered in prayer.

chapter six

TIME OUT

When Atatürk established the Republic of Turkey, he changed the day of rest from the Islamic Friday to the Western Sunday. The working week runs from Monday to Friday for banks and offices, and from Monday to Saturday for shops. Lots of shops and restaurants are open on Sunday, too. Religious people may take a long lunchtime on Friday to go to the mosque for the holiest prayer time of the week; a small business owner may close his shop or business during this Friday lunch period.

SHOPPING

From crowded bazaars to high-tech shopping malls, Turkey is a country where you can shop till you drop. Turks go to shopping centers as a pastime. Window-shopping in the beautiful and fashionable malls of Istanbul, which rank among the best in the world, can be a pleasure. Visitors should experience the colorful and exciting bazaars, both the local, open-air markets and the grand old covered markets where they can find clothing, spices, fresh fruit and vegetables, and traditional ceramic wares, rugs, gold, and jewelry.

In bazaars it is usual to bargain; you may end up paying about half the original asking price. When trying out your bargaining skills, it is best to get a rough feel for the real value of the goods before you start, then venture an offer of half that price. Don't start to haggle unless you have a real intention of buying the goods if the shopkeeper comes down in price. It is very rude to strike a deal through bargaining and then not buy. Also, specify your method of payment early on. *Nakit* means cash, and you can get a better deal for cash than with a credit card. Shopping centers have fixed prices—don't try to negotiate in the supermarket or in a luxury shop.

Shopping can be an enjoyable social experience, and Turkish women dress well for the occasion. Don't expect to dash into a shop, buy what you need, and dash out: small shopkeepers will offer you tea and expect to chat. Note that even if you get a good deal, your Turkish friends will always say they could have got it for you more cheaply—so why not ask them to come shopping with you? They will enjoy helping you to get a good price.

Shops in Turkey stay open late into the evening, often until 9:00 or 10:00 p.m. (bazaars close at sundown), are generally open on Saturday, and many also on Sunday. There are special neighborhoods for certain goods in each town: there will be a bookshop district, a lighting district, a street of clothes shops, a street with hardware products or car parts. There are many well-respected Turkish and international stores with branches throughout the country, such as Boyner and YKM department stores, Carrefour, Real and Migros supermarkets, Beymen, Marks & Spencer, Zara, and Toys"R"Us. One shop of particular interest is Vakko; this family-owned department store sells women's scarves and men's ties made of high-quality silk, featuring designs from Turkish textiles and mosaics or reproductions of contemporary Turkish art.

Leather goods and gold are both very reasonable. Gold is priced by weight; the market price changes daily, and is printed in the newspaper just like a currency exchange rate. The vendor will weigh your chosen piece, and calculate the price from today's market value. Other great gift items and souvenirs to buy are copper, silverware, and glassware.

Carpets are a must buy! You'll find a great selection and many different regional designs. They vary in quality: exquisite silk from the town of Hereke, or wool, machine, or handmade. When purchasing a carpet, remember that the more knots per square centimeter, the more expensive the carpet will be. You get what you pay for. Carpet buying can be a long process, with the owner showing you every carpet in the shop, rolling them out with panache. Don't try to skip this stage: a carpet is not a cheap item, and

you are entitled to see the full range. You will be offered a lot of tea in the process. Point out the carpets you like, and these will be set aside for you to look at again later. It is acceptable to try to bargain.

People will try to sell you antiques. In particular, boys will approach you as you tour old ruins, offering you little pots or old coins. Be careful, because these cannot be taken out of the country legally. There are strict laws governing the export of antiquities and artifacts such as coins, pottery, jewelry, paintings, and carpets.

Tour guides get a commission from the shops they recommend. Take time to look around; cross the street to see a shop that will not be paying your guide a commission, and may give you a discount. Also, when meeting Turks in the street in tourist areas, remember that, "my uncle has a good shop" probably means, "I am employed by a particular shopkeeper to approach tourists and take them to his shop." Use your own judgment.

CHANGING YOUR MONEY

In general it is better not to exchange much money before traveling to Turkey, as you can often get a better rate there. All cities have a large number of banks and ATM machines. Banks are open from 9:00 a.m. to 4:00 p.m., Monday to Friday, with most of them closing between 12:30 and 1:30 p.m. for lunch. International banks HSBC and ING Bank are in Turkey, and many good Turkish banks also exist.

The easiest way to change money is at the *döviz*, a licensed money changer. *Döviz* bureaus are small, main-street premises; they are regulated and often give the best rates. Rates will be posted on boards (so compare if two or three *döviz* bureaus are near to each other) and the posted rate is what you get, with no extra commission. US dollars, euros, and sterling are the most widely traded foreign currencies. Most hotels will change money, but they give a worse rate than the bank or *döviz*. Beware of money changers on the street. At best you may get a poor rate; at worst you may end up with counterfeit notes.

Traveler's checks are almost impossible to exchange and attract a high commission. Credit cards are widely accepted in shops and restaurants. Visa and Mastercard are the easiest to use; often shops are not equipped to process other credit cards, or debit cards. Beware of fraud—it is best not to use your card in a small backstreet outfit. Many shops and hotels accept US dollars, euros, and sterling.

FOOD AND DRINK

Turkish cuisine is one of the many joys awaiting the visitor. There are luscious fruits and vegetables in season, stuffed with rice, raisins, pine nuts, or meat, nourishing stews, and on the coasts, freshly cooked fish straight from the sea.

Turkish cooks are as concerned with presentation as with flavor. Traditionally, as many as two hundred different spices were used for a meal, providing color and an abundance of flavor. A Turkish saying reads "First appeal to the eyes, then fill the stomach."

Lamb is the most popular meat. Beef, often grilled as a kebab, is common, as is chicken, especially prepared with walnuts, paprika, and garlic. Meat is prepared according to Islamic (Halal) rules, which prohibit the eating of pork, ham, bacon, and other pig products. You may find them at an exclusive restaurant or five-star hotel, but they are not generally available in Turkey.

Rice is usually served, sometimes with currants, pine nuts, and spices. Much fresh produce is home grown. Garlic and olives are used widely, as with much Mediterranean cuisine. Food tends to be seasonal, due to the emphasis on fresh ingredients.

Eating Out

Turks are passionate about food. Snacks can be purchased everywhere; sellers roam the streets carrying a flat board loaded with tasty wares on their head. Buffets and kiosks line the roadside, and glass-sided pushcarts display other savories.

Commonly enjoyed snacks are nuts and sunflower seeds, sweetcorn, *simit* (sesame-coated bread rings), *kokoreç* (grilled sheep's intestine), fresh fish sandwiches, fried mussels on a stick, and meatballs. In contrast, there is also a wide range of international fast-food chains.

Late nights are common, and Turks thoroughly enjoy going out on the town, as families, in groups,

or on their own. There are restaurants and cafés to satisfy every palate, from regional fish to meat, pastry shops to delicatessens, and even sushi bars in the trendy urban centers. Turks generally have supper around 7:30 or 8:30 p.m.

Don't be shy when it comes to choosing Turkish food; you can often inspect the kitchen, ask questions, and point to what you want.

The Turkish dining experience may be one of the most memorable events of your trip. A typical restaurant meal will contain the following courses, with the starters (one cold and one hot) consisting of assorted small dishes on individual plates.

Meze (Cold Starters)
Usually a tray with ten or so varieties will be shown to you. Typical selections include stuffed vine leaves or green peppers (*dolma*), cheese, vegetables such as eggplant or okra in olive oil, spicy tomato paste, eggplant and watercress

folded in garlic yogurt, chickpea paste (hummus), potato salad, and cracked wheat in tomato and chili sauce (*kısır*). There is also usually delicious fresh bread.

Salata (Salad)
Fresh fruit and vegetables are wonderful in Turkey. The two most common types of salad are a "shepherd's salad" (*çoban salatası*) of chopped

tomatoes, cucumbers, and onions, and a "seasonal salad" (*mevsim salatası*) of lettuce, grated carrots or red cabbage, tomato and cucumber slices, sweetcorn, and green peppers.

Çorba (Soup)

You must taste red lentil soup (*mercimek*), yogurt and rice soup (*yayla*), or tomato (*domates*), chicken (*tavuk*), or mushroom (*mantar*) soups. Tripe soup (*işkembe)* has a strong smell and is an acquired taste. Soups are often enhanced by freshly squeezed lemon or sweet red pepper fried in butter.

Ara Sıcak (Hot Starters)

Here you can choose from such delights as deep-fried cheese pastry roll (*sigara böreği*), deep-fried balls of rice, mince, and nuts (*içli köfte*), calamari (*kalamar*), and fried mussels (*midye*).

Et (Meat Dishes)

Kebab means "small pieces of meat." "Shish kebab" (*şiş*) is pieces of meat roasted on a skewer. A *döner* (literally meaning "it turns") is lamb or chicken grilled on a rotating spit. *Döner kebab* is slices of this meat served in bread as a sandwich (*ekmek arası*), wrapped in thin pastry (*dürüm*), or on a plate with vegetables. *Köfte* is meatballs made from ground meat, parsley, and bread or rice. Steaks are

available, but Turks normally like them well done. "Rare" in Turkey normally corresponds to "medium" elsewhere. Chicken is not traditional, but can be found in most preparations, even as a schnitzel. There are various dishes special to regions of Turkey. *İskender kebabı* is slices of lamb served with tomato sauce and yogurt; Adana kebabs are not spicy, and Urfa kebabs are. Other specialty meat dishes to look for are *sarma beyti*, chunks of meat wrapped around with thin pastry, and *babaganuş*, chunks of meat served on a bed of eggplant pureed with garlic and lemon. Turkish cuisine is easily adaptable for vegetarians.

Balık (Fish)
Fish is best eaten fresh at coastal or lakeside restaurants. It is normally steamed (*buharlı*), grilled (*tava*), or fried (*kızartma*). Popular choices, depending on the time of year, include anchovy (*hamsi*), sea bass (*levrek*), blue fish (*lüfer*), bream (*çipura*), turbot (*kalkan*), and mackerel (*uskumru*).

It is a good idea to ask the waiter which fish is freshest and in season.

Pide (Turkish Pizza)

Unlike its Italian cousin, Turkish *pide* does not have tomato sauce, nor is it round but rather long and rolled at the edges. The soft pastry base is topped with white or cheddar cheese, and then, if you wish, meat, spinach, or egg. *Lahmacun* is a special variety of ground meat with tomato and onion sauce on a very thin pastry base. It is rolled and eaten with parsley or chopped lettuce inside.

Tatlı (Dessert)

Turkish dessert is usually very sticky. Try filo pastry soaked in syrup and sprinkled with nuts (*baklava*), a similar dish made with shredded wheat (*kadayıf*),

quince in syrup (*ayva tatlısı*), or pumpkin in syrup (*kabak tatlısı*). Alternatives to syrupy desserts are milk pudding (*muhalebe*) or rice pudding (*sütlaç*). Turkish delight (*lokum*) made from rose water, pistachios, coconut, and powdered sugar, is eaten as a dessert or with coffee. It travels well and makes a great gift item.

Regional Specialties

Turkish food varies from region to region. Some specialties can be traced back to the nomadic tribesmen of Central Asia: for example, *sucuk* and *pastırma* are forms of spicy cured meat, originally made by putting the meat under the saddle. Pressure from the weight of the rider and salt from the horse's sweat would preserve it.

The southeast has a spicier diet. When urban Turks are on a journey they will stop and buy foods special to each town: for example, Susurluk *ayran* (yogurt drink), Bursa candied chestnuts and peaches, Black Sea hazelnuts and fresh anchovies, Izmit *pişmaniye* (spun sugar), Antep pistachios, and Afyon spicy sausage.

Drinking

Restaurants may or may not serve alcohol, depending on their ownership and their proximity to schools. If they do, then often local (*yerli*) brands are much cheaper than imported (*ithal*) versions of beer, gin, or wine. Most local alcohol is produced by the state monopoly. Turkish beer is like lager, rather than British ale. It is served cold. A common brand is Efes (Ephesus) beer, which comes in normal, light, and dark varieties. Turkey has a good range of red and white wines; two of the main vineyards are Doluca and Kavaklıdere. Wine is drunk mainly by the middle and upper classes, and all alcohol drinks are frowned upon by conservative Muslims. During Ramadan, out of deference, some restaurants that would normally serve alcohol will not do so. A law passed in 2013 bans the sale of alcohol after 10:00 p.m. in shops.

Turks love to sit in cafés and chat with their friends. The national alcoholic drink is *rakı*, an aniseed-flavored spirit similar to the Greek *ouzo* that is mixed with water until it turns cloudy. It is

also referred to as "lion's milk." The *rakı* table is a ceremonial meal; the *rakı* is drunk with a wide array of hot and cold appetizers.

Strong tea is drunk everywhere. It is normally served in a small, tulip-shaped glass with no milk and usually sweet. Tea is the universal Turkish offering to guests and friends. It is polite to ask for weak tea. Just say "*açık olsun.*" Your glass will be refilled many times. If you do not want any more, place the teaspoon over the top of the glass.

Famous throughout the world, Turkish coffee is drunk in a small cup and is very black and strong. Some phrases for describing how you like your coffee are *sade*, no sugar; *az şekerli*, slightly sweetened; *orta*, medium-sweet; and *çok şekerli*, very sweet. Good Turkish coffee is frothy on top. Drink only halfway down, and be careful not to swirl the cup or you will get the unpleasant-tasting grounds. A Turkish proverb about friendship and coffee reads "A cup of coffee commits the drinker to forty years of friendship." On a hot day, try the refreshing *ayran*, which is yogurt and water mixed.

TABLE MANNERS

Usually in public eating places there is a family salon—women or children do not sit in an area designated for men. The old picture of a Turkish restaurant full of cigarette smoke is a thing of the past. Smokers by law now have to sit outside, a change that has led to many restaurants having glassed-in patios to cater for their patrons who wish to smoke.

Table manners vary. Generally, Turks hold the fork in the right hand and the knife in the left, and do not switch them. There are some strict Muslims who do not use the left hand for eating at all. The table may be laid by placing the cutlery crossed on the plate. Turks do not rest one hand on their lap while eating; both hands are kept above the table. When you have finished, place your knife and fork side by side on your plate. Waiters attentively whisk away the empty dishes (hold on to your glass if you are still drinking), and may also remove your plate or cutlery at any time and give you clean ones.

A meal is often part of doing business. If you have been invited, always accept, and don't try to split the cost if your host insists on paying—he would say that you would pay for him if he were in your home town. If appropriate, you can reciprocate later.

When you are are ready to pay, it always works to pretend to scribble on your hand to signal to the waiter that you want the bill. When it comes, be sure to check it. A tip of 10 percent is usual.

TIPS (BAHŞIŞ)

Employees are often paid the minimum wage, and expect tips. Always tip in cash.

Restaurant: 10 percent (not usually added in, unless the menu says so)

Taxi: 10 percent if the ride has been good (typically, round the fare up to the higher TL)

Airport: fixed tariff for baggage (check signs)

Bell boy: US $1–2 per bag. For other tips at a hotel, there is usually a box in reception for all staff: US $5–10

Tour guides: approx. US $2 per person in the group. Same for the driver.

Barber, beauty parlor, Turkish bath: about 10 percent, split between the people who have helped you (it is often acceptable to tuck the money into their pocket).

Car park attendant outside hotel or restaurant: if there is no parking fee and the attendant brings your car to the door, tip US $2–3 (more if yours is a luxury car!)

LEISURE

Turks love to window-shop in the winter and be outside in the summer, and enjoy strolling in parks and on the beach. There are plenty of things to do and see in the major urban areas.

Music

The Turks love music. Those who can afford it go to concerts. Major cities have cultural events with international stars and local performers. Turkish classical music is very distinctive. The rhythm and scale are typically Middle Eastern, and the music is in a choral, folk ballad style. There may be a full choir, or just a solo singer. Typical instruments include the *kanun* (a zitherlike instrument with seventy-two strings), *tambur* (a long-necked stringed instrument similar to the mandolin), *ud* (like a lute), *ney* (a reed flute), and *saz* (a small lute). Turkish music is  filled with emotion and expression, which usually gets the audience swaying and singing along. Live entertainment in restaurants includes some traditional folk songs (*fasıl*).

Every year there are privately sponsored music and film festivals in Istanbul. A variety of music such as jazz, classical, and popular is performed.

Popular music consists of Western-style Turkish pop. This has a lively rhythm that sets your feet dancing and hips and shoulders swaying, but is again based on the Middle Eastern scale of notes. Turks will love it if you know the names of popular artists. Sertab Erener won the Eurovision Song Contest in 2003, with a great example of Turkish pop music, "Every Way That I Can."

On public transportation or in taxis, the driver will often listen to what Turks call "Arabesque" songs, typically lamenting the treachery of a loved one, or a case of unrequited love.

Cinema

Turkish films are very dramatic—the plot nearly always includes gun chases and romance. They always have a sad ending.

All of the latest Hollywood films are shown at your local cinema. Normally films will be in their original language, with Turkish subtitles. The only exception to this is children's films, which will be dubbed. Halfway through the film, there will be an abrupt break. The film reel has not snapped—this is the mandatory ten-minute break to allow the Turkish cinemagoers to enjoy their cigarettes.

Dance

In Turkey this encompasses regional folk dances and folklore, classical ballet, and modern dance. *Halay* is a well-known folk dance performed in a circle, accompanied by a drum or pipe.

The belly dance is synonymous with Turkey, although it did not originate there, but elsewhere in the Middle East. The specially trained dancers are called *dansöz*. A dancer may be hired to perform at a private party for a wedding or birthday celebration; others appear regularly as part of a cabaret in a club, or at special shows put on for tourists. Turks of both sexes and all ages appreciate the skill and training of a top dancer, and will show their appreciation of a good dancer by clapping along and tucking a note under her bra strap when she passes their table. She will share this money with the music group. The most fervent admirers of the belly dancers will not always be male; there will often be older women in raincoats and headscarves cheering the scantily clad girl from the front row.

Humor
The Turks have a good sense of humor and can poke fun at themselves and others. Nasrettin Hoca ("Hodja") and Temel from the Black Sea region are famous characters in jokes. Nasrettin Hoca's jokes are clever stories that expose the shortcomings of society in an ingenuous kind of way. Temel jokes project an image of simple country folk—Temel is always the idiot who makes a major mistake.

Puppetry
Karagöz and Hacivat are shadow puppets, dressed in Ottoman dress. This is a folk art tradition, and is not just for children. Their plays are comic political satire. Karagöz (the village idiot) says the wrong words and gets hold of the wrong end of the stick. Hacivat is bright and always sets him straight. This traditional art form is often updated to poke fun at modern public figures and issues.

SPORTS
The National Game

Turkish men don't just love football (that is, soccer)—they are crazy about it. Every street is a football field in the summer. If you would like to support one of the well-known teams, here are some tips. The best teams are Beşiktaş (The Eagles), Istanbul, black and white; Fenerbahçe (The Canaries), Istanbul, navy and yellow; Galatasaray (The Lions), Istanbul, red and yellow (chant: "Cim Bom Bom"); Trabzonspor (The Tigers), Trabzon, maroon and blue.

Turkey has been successful in Europe and the World Cup. Turks will ask whom you support, and you'll impress them if you are knowledgeable about their teams. They are certainly well-informed about European teams. Fans are fanatical. Every soccer game is like a festival, with firecrackers and drums.

Other Sports

Basketball is popular. Gyms are everywhere in the major urban areas. Indoor swimming pools are becoming more common but are generally found only in major hotels. Some tennis courts are available for a fee. Turks are becoming more aware of health—a few even jog. Jogging is unusual, particularly for women, except among the middle and upper classes.

Skiing is possible during the winter months at Uludağ near Bursa, Kartalkaya near Bolu, Palandöken near Erzurum, and Saklıkent in Antalya. It is expensive and crowded on weekends.

If you like to play golf, there are some country clubs on the outskirts of Istanbul, or golf resorts near Antalya. This, too, is very expensive due to the cost of upkeep of the greens in a hot country.

Lottery and Gambling
The national lottery is called Milli Piyango, and the largest jackpots are at New Year and other national holidays. It seems that nearly everybody buys a ticket in the hope of winning something. There is a one in five chance that you will win the *amorti* and get your ticket money back. The winning numbers are printed in the newspapers. Instant lottery and a pools system of gambling on the results of football matches are also available.

Casino-style gambling was made illegal by a government with strong Islamic sympathies a few years ago, and all the casinos in Turkey were closed down. Those who like to indulge fly to northern Cyprus, where every major hotel has a large casino attached. Often at least half of the passengers on the flights from Istanbul to Ercan, Cyprus, are groups of rich elderly widows. They get their enjoyment from gambling some of their inheritance with their friends, and why not? Their trip to Cyprus is paid for by the hotel if they pledge to spend a minimum amount in the casino.

THE *HAMAM*
Hamam is the Turkish word for the traditional bathhouse. In the olden days, people did not have baths in their houses, but went to the *hamam*. In

Ottoman times it was the center of gossip and social activity. Some people still think of it as a social center. Nowadays it is mainly used on special occasions (for example, as part of a bride's prenuptial preparations) or by curious tourists.

Men and women have separate sections in the *hamam*. You will be given the essentials: a large towel (*peştemal*) that you tie around your waist to protect your modesty, special wooden block shoes, and a bowl. You bring your own soap. The bathing room is very steamy. There are sinks around the walls, and a channel of water runs round the perimeter. You choose your spot, and sit on the marble floor in front of a sink with hot and cold taps. You fill your bowl and pour the water over yourself. Turks believe that water should be running—to sit in a tub of water is unclean. Part of the experience is to get really clean by exfoliating the top layer of dead skin. For best results don't use soap until you have been exfoliated. Plenty of hot water on the skin means you can rub this layer off with a special sponge, or have a masseur/masseuse do this for you.

In the steam room you wash, and you can have a vigorous massage while lying on a heated slab of marble. Everything is marble, and hot. The whole bath area has under-floor heating. If you feel it will be your only chance, go for the whole works (the rub with rough gloves, the soaping, and the face and feet massages).

There is a Turkish proverb, "*Hamama giren terler,*" "He who goes into a *hamam* will sweat." If you don't like the heat, get out!

VISITING A MOSQUE

Each neighborhood takes pride in having a beautiful mosque—the spiritual focus of the community. It represents a combination of art and spirituality. The graceful, slender minarets lead the eye heavenward, and the interior, too, provides a feast for the eyes, from the intricate calligraphic designs on the walls to the patterned carpets stretching across the floor.

You may be asked to enter through a separate doorway. Visitors are not allowed during prayer time. Men should not go into the section reserved for women. Be respectful, and cover up; in the mosques frequented by tourists, there are wraps for women with too-short skirts or men with shorts. Women must cover their heads. Everyone is expected to leave their shoes outside.

chapter seven

TRAVEL, HEALTH, & SAFETY

With its magnificent climate, long Aegean and Mediterranean coastlines, and wonderful history, Turkey is a great vacation destination. Every type of vacation can be found here. The young can enjoy a beach vacation with magnificent scenery and lively nightlife. History buffs will find an amazing range of archaeological ruins. Backpackers can explore beautiful scenery and discover remote parts of the country.

Tourist information offices are operated by the Ministry of Tourism. Every Turkish city and town has one, and in Istanbul there are branch offices in each of the major tourist sites. You can obtain free brochures, maps, and helpful information.

ROADS AND TRAFFIC

Paradoxically, in a country where regulations, bureaucracy, and standing in line mean that things in general take a long time, Turkish drivers are in an amazing hurry. They are risk takers, and often appear aggressive.

In Turkey you drive on the right. There have been great improvements to the main road network. However, heavy traffic, speeding, poor signaling

accompanied by risky overtaking, potholes, and unclear signposts generally make driving a challenge. Urban rush hour is not for the fainthearted. Fast jeeps, trucks, old tractors, and the occasional donkey cart share the same roads.

Westerners will need to learn a different driving etiquette. The use of the horn is not always negative. It can mean "hurry up," "watch out," "hello," "do you want a lift?," and so on. Drivers do not always stick to the designated lane and may create a new one, and often turn without signaling. In a Turkish car the indicator light rarely wears out—but the horn is sure to!

Turkish traffic lights have some interesting features. Many have been fitted with a countdown showing how many seconds there are till the light changes. This enables traffic near a green light to speed up to get through just in time before the light changes, or cars stopped at red to rev their engines ready to peel off the second the light changes. The definition of a nanosecond in Turkey is the time it takes between the traffic light turning green and the driver behind hooting because you haven't moved yet. Traffic lights often have no amber, but, curiously, at night they can be switched off and just flash amber.

To survive driving in Turkey you must learn to be assertive. While there are rules for who has the right of way (for example, on a traffic circle, priority is for vehicles joining from the right), this is in practice based on who gets their nose out first. Drivers tend to be impatient and reluctant to back up if another car comes head-on in a narrow street. Traffic rules are flagrantly flouted, but if you get caught you will be fined and will receive penalty points on your license.

On intercity routes, speed traps with radar are routine. The speed limits are strictly 31 mph (50 kmph) in cities, 56 mph (90 kmph) on open road (62 mph/100 kmph on divided highways), and 75 mph (120 kmph) on expressways.

If you do have an accident, generally whoever hits the other car is at fault, even if it pulled out without looking. So be ready to make an emergency stop at all times. If you have an accident a report must be submitted to the police before insurance will honor the claim. You may have to wait a long time before the police arrive. The cars should not be moved. Other drivers involved in the accident may not want to wait and will leave (possibly because they don't want to be caught without insurance or a valid car tax stamp). Wait, even if you cause a ten-mile traffic jam! Leaving the scene is punishable by a fine.

Don't confuse Turkish driving etiquette with your own. The flashing of headlights doesn't mean

"You go first." It means "Don't even think about it: I'm going."

The main expressway going from Bulgaria through Istanbul and Ankara (the TEM), the two Istanbul bridges, and some other roads are toll roads. You can no longer pay by cash at these tolls. Just by each toll station is a small building where you can buy a card for either the HGS or KGS system that will give you a certain number of toll entrances. It can be topped up when necessary.

Drinking and Driving

Driving under the influence of alcohol is illegal. There are not many random breath tests, but you will be tested routinely if you are involved in an accident, even if it was not your fault. There are strict penalties also for driving under the influence of alcohol—the legal limit is 1.0 promille.

Car and Driver's License

Foreigners can drive on a foreign license, but if you are to be resident for a while you must get a Turkish license from Turing (the Turkish Driving Association). In practice, this law is not often applied, although some insurance companies are requiring it. If you do not do this, and if your license doesn't have a photo, it is a good idea to get it translated by a notary public. Otherwise, a traffic policeman who does not speak English may not accept it.

When purchasing insurance, it is for the car, not the driver. There are two types: *Zorunlu trafik* is mandatory and gives low protection; *Kasko* is fully comprehensive coverage.

INTERCITY TRAVEL

Planes

Turkish Airlines (THY) has a good network connecting all the major cities. Flight times range from one hour for Istanbul to Ankara to two hours from Istanbul to Diyarbakır. Some flights require changing planes in Ankara or Istanbul. Passengers should always travel with ID—this can be your passport or some other form of valid identification. Prices are reasonable: domestic flights cost around US $150–200 return. Flights are nonsmoking. Normally, a soft drink and a sandwich are served on board.

Discount airlines such as Pegasus and Atlas Jet operate a wide network of flights in competition with THY. THY has responded by developing its own discount carrier—Anadolu Jet. Be sure to check all the Web sites for a great deal before buying.

Buses

Before flights became cheaper, the road network was the main means of intercity travel in Turkey. Expressways are limited; many are just divided highways. After planes, buses are the next best way to travel around the country if you have time. It is to the traveler's advantage that there is competition between private companies. You can book a ticket or just turn up at an out-of-town bus station and hop on. Go to the office of the bus company—if you don't know which to choose, you will be sure to be accosted by men trying to get you to use their company!

Travel between Istanbul and Ankara can take as little as four hours. Many buses travel at night (for example, twenty hours for Istanbul to Trabzon, nine hours for Istanbul to Izmir). Some companies have a better safety record than others: Kamil Koç, Ulusoy, and Varan are regarded as the best. They target the more wealthy traveler; on some routes, onboard toilets and meals are provided. On other routes there will be regular stops at service stations or bus stations. Buses are nonsmoking.

Trains

The traditional train network is very limited and is slow and uncomfortable. Even the Istanbul to Ankara "express" train stops many times and takes about nine hours. But there is currently a large program of investment in the railways. A high-speed rail link that will soon link Istanbul and Ankara is open between Eskişehir and Ankara. Plans to roll out high-speed links from the capital to cities such as Konya are also underway.

Ferries

You can get an overnight ferry from Istanbul to Izmir, but it is not recommended as the cabin

accommodation is fairly basic and it takes about twelve hours. The fast ferry across the Marmara Sea from Istanbul to Yalova, Marmara Island, Bandırma, and other destinations is by catamaran and is much better. A travel network of these "sea buses" is being developed.

Crossing the Road

Pedestrians need nerves of steel. It is best to cross at traffic lights (many lights have a countdown for pedestrians as well), but still check both ways that all traffic has stopped. Don't be fooled into thinking that black and white stripes on the road mean you have the right of way as a pedestrian. Crossing the street is dangerous. Whenever possible, use a footbridge or underpass (the latter often has nice kiosks and shops).

LOCAL TRANSPORTATION
Buses

These buses are operated by the local authority. There are two types: in one you buy a ticket beforehand, in the other you pay on board. Buses have set routes, with set stops. Some cities have *akbil*, a prepaid electronic ticket that deducts a credit each time you use it. You can buy a monthly pass giving unlimited travel. Bus drivers can drive fast and brake quickly. Always try to sit; if this is not possible, stand where you can brace yourself. There is usually no standing allowed on Havaş buses. They run from the airport to the city center, and are often the cheapest and simplest option.

Minibuses

Private minibuses are licensed by the local authority. There is a set minibus route. The difference between a bus and minibus is that you can hail and ride; the minibus does not have defined stops, and you can hop on and off where you like along the route. The first time you ride a minibus you may wonder what is going on when everyone behind you keeps saying something and then passing money up to you, to the front. You pay on the minibus by passing your fare up the row of passengers. Your change will come back to you from the driver in the same way.

When you want to get off, say, so that the driver can hear you, "*İnecek var*" ("I want to get off").

Dolmuş

A dolmuş is a special shared taxi. It has a fixed route, generally shorter than the minibus, and departs when it is full. It is a little more expensive than a minibus but usually quicker. Say the phrase above when you want to get out.

Local Ferries

The ferry is a common way of crossing the Bosporus in Istanbul, or crossing the bay in Izmir. Istanbul's sea transport is run by IDO (Istanbul Deniz Otobüsleri A.Ş.). Entry to the ferry station is via a turnstile; you can use an *akbil* or buy a token called a *jeton* from a booth at the entrance to the ferry station. Once the ferry has docked and passengers have disembarked, the gate is opened and you go out on to the pier. Don't copy the experienced Turks and leap across the water! Wait to use the gangplank, even though this is usually just a narrow plank of wood. Enjoy the view from the ferry in nice weather; you can have tea and *simit* (sesame-coated bread ring) or a hot *sahlep* (orchis root) drink on board.

Istanbul also has a network of sea buses (catamaran fast ferries) linking the shores of the Bosporus and the coasts of the Marmara Sea. These run less frequently than the regular ferries, and are more expensive, but the ride is quicker, the seating more luxurious, and boarding and disembarking are definitely safer.

Taxis

It is best to use licensed taxis, not private ones. All official taxis in the major cities are yellow and have a license plate beginning T. It is best to use the taxi *durak* (stand), or to use a taxi called from the stand by the receptionist of the office, hotel, or restaurant where you have been, because if there is any problem you can contact the stand manager. However, you can hail one easily at the roadside.

Normally the passenger gets in the back. If your group is more than two people and is mixed, women go in the back and a man in front. All taxis should have a *saat* (meter). You pay by distance and by time, so the meter will tick over if you are stuck in traffic (common in big cities). It is usual to tip 10 percent.

If you know the route you'd like to take, you can tell the taxi driver; otherwise he may choose a longer route. Remember that face-saving is a Turkish trait—if a taxi driver is lost he may not want to admit this and may ask a passerby. (Even if he did he could get the wrong directions, as the passerby would not want to admit to not knowing either.) Taxi drivers love to talk.

Trams/Metro
Trams and metro routes are springing up in cities across Turkey. These are quick modes of transport, but the networks may not cover the whole town or city. Entrance to both is via a turnstile, operated by an *akbil* or a *jeton* token purchased from a little booth nearby.

WHERE TO STAY

Every town has a range of hotels and cheaper *pansiyons* (guest houses or hostels). Even in the smallest towns, hotels range from one-star to at least three-star. Although there are walk-in rates posted, you can try to negotiate a price. Check that the price is inclusive (*dahil*) of tax (KDV) and breakfast (*kahvaltı*).

In a small town, or in a lower-class hotel, check that everything in the room works before you agree to stay. It is normal to ask to see the room first. Four- and five-star hotels have business facilities such as satellite TV, meeting rooms, and Internet connection, and are likely to have a sports and leisure center. Remember that the minibar and calls from the room are expensive.

You will need to show ID (normally a passport) to check in. If you don't pay at check-in, they will keep your ID until you check out.

HEALTH

There are some standard dos and don'ts to keeping well during your stay in Turkey. In general, don't drink tap water, or water or lemonade sold from a pitcher on the street. Bottled water is always best. Avoid uncooked foods such as salads, unless you are in a home or a good quality hotel or restaurant. If you get a bad cut you must have a tetanus shot. Watch out for hepatitis and HIV in your activities; these are present but there is little public awareness of them.

If you get sunstroke, and your blood pressure falls and you feel faint, a good remedy is the yogurt drink *ayran*, as it has a high level of salt.

Good health care is available in the private sector. There are private hospitals and clinics in towns and cities. If you are taken ill in a rural area it would be a good idea to go to the nearest large town for treatment. Private hospitals have state of the art technology, with many medical staff trained abroad. They are well-informed about the latest treatments and may be fluent in English or German. Although state hospitals are improving, in smaller locations they are best avoided. The ambulance service is private, and often each hospital has its own ambulance; be aware that this can mean an ambulance team will take you to its own hospital and not necessarily to the nearest one. The emergency department is called *Acil Servis*. Insurance is advised: show this at entry. Usually if you have a foreign insurance policy you will have to pay by credit card at the hospital, keep the receipt, and claim later.

In big cities many foreign drugs are available, most without prescription, so you can buy them over the counter at a pharmacy (*eczane*). The pharmacist can also check your blood pressure or cholesterol level, give injections, and so on.

SAFETY

Travelers who dress and behave respectably are as safe in Turkey as anywhere in the world. Violent crime is not usually random; most violent crimes are crimes of passion, or retribution for a serious affront. Football games can generate violence.

Foreign women who have moved to Istanbul from large cities in the USA or Europe often say they feel safer walking in the street in the evenings in Istanbul than back home. If you are a woman traveling alone or two women late at night it is best not to attract attention to yourself. It is usually assumed that you are trying to invite male company. If you are careful you will be fine. In seaside resorts or tourist areas some Turkish men make a living by picking up Western women and showing them the town, at the women's expense.

Western women, particularly Americans, are often misunderstood because of their openness. Honest curiosity or light conversation may be interpreted as flirtation. Turkish men generally are not used to much interaction with women they don't know. Although mixed group activities are common at school and work, it is improper for a Turkish man to show too much interest in a woman without getting to know her through his family or social circle first. He might think that a foreign woman is open to his advances. If you feel uncomfortable, tell another Turk in the group that he is too friendly for your liking. They will know how to deal with it and will be pleased to help.

Turkish men have a justified reputation for being Casanovas, and if you go out alone with a Turk he is likely to assume that you will be open to his amorous approaches.

During the 1990s, the southeast of the country experienced considerable unrest. These troubles are now under control, and the area is once again open to cultural and historical tours. There have been sporadic acts of terror in large cities such as Istanbul, but this is no more heightened than in many European cities. It is wise to obtain up-to-date information from your government before travel. Long-term residents should register with their embassy if they live in Ankara, or consulate if they live in other large cities. The consulates provide regular updates on such matters.

Shoplifting and pickpocketing increased during the economic slump, especially in the tourist and market areas. Be careful if people try to distract you or follow you—they may be petty thieves after your wallet or cash. Sometimes a person may approach you to change money on the street. Decline—it is often counterfeit.

chapter eight

BUSINESS BRIEFING

Turkey is a rapidly developing country with sophisticated facilities in its major towns and cities. The economy used to be based on agriculture, mining and quarrying of raw materials such as coal and marble, and simple manufacturing; today it is much more diversified. Still a major exporter of crops such as dates, figs, nuts, and citrus fruit, and raw materials such as marble, Turkey is also a world leader in the manufacture of textiles and automobiles, and has a growing service sector.

Turks are very hospitable, and your business hosts will look after you. Turkey is used to international practices, and many of the hotels, restaurants, and offices in the major cities are as good as any in the West. You can easily keep up to date with CNN and BBC World when traveling.

Business hours are typically from 9:00 a.m. to 6:00 p.m., Monday to Friday. Shops are open late, and on Saturday and Sunday. Holiday months are July and August, and the week of *Şeker Bayramı* and *Kurban Bayramı*.

OFFICE ETIQUETTE AND PROTOCOL

When doing business with Turks keep in mind their key values. Preserving honor and saving face, both for oneself and for the other party, are paramount. People and relationships are more important than time, and making contacts is the key to success. Networking is the foundation of business in Turkey. Many foreigners fail to realize that this is how business happens: time spent building relationships is not wasted, but opens doors to future success.

The best way to build a network is to develop a relationship with someone who already has good contacts. You will then be introduced as a friend. Making this first contact will involve investing time in getting to know the other party, calling them regularly, asking how things are going for them, and generally being helpful.

A possible starting point is a trade fair. Turkey has many of these, and they are an opportunity to meet potential clients, partners, and distributors. Take advantage of social opportunities and be sure to follow up quickly and frequently with a call. Another useful route is to join trade delegations organized by government agencies or international chambers of commerce. International banks and accountancy firms can also give advice on how to do business and build contacts.

Business Cards

Business cards are widely used. Those who work for multinationals may have dual-language cards, with their title and details in Turkish on one side and in English on the reverse. When people give you their business cards, treat them with respect. Carry a small cardholder to keep them in.

Your Turkish contact may have put an ink cross mark on the back of his or her card. This practice stems from the fact that it was common to write an amount of money on the back of a business card as a pledge. The cross cancelled it.

Business Gifts

In business, gifts are given at *bayram* (official holidays). These are normally quite smart: perhaps a monogrammed diary or desk set, or a basket of choice food or preserves.

MEETINGS

Professional occasions require punctuality. Due to the vagaries of traffic in Istanbul, however, it is acceptable to be slightly late as long as you call on your cell phone to say you are stuck in traffic.

A business meeting usually begins with tea and an introductory chat about the participants' health, their families, and the general state of business, the economy, and the world. Ten or fifteen minutes can pass before getting down to the point of the meeting. Wait for your contact to broach the subject. In time, you will be asked in detail about your company, products, services, and competitors. Only at this point is it appropriate to start talking business.

Formal address is used. In a professional setting, a person's given name will never be used on its own. Your Turkish partners will typically add "Miss" or "Mr." to the given name, addressing you as Mr. John rather than Mr. Smith, but never John. You may refer to a Turk as Mr. Ahmet or Miss Ayşe, but it is also acceptable to say "Ahmet Bey" or "Ayşe Hanım." If you speak Turkish, use the formal *siz*, not the *sen* second-person form of the verb, even if you know the person quite well.

Protocol is important, and there is a strict hierarchy. Respect should be given to those in a senior position. The face-saving aspect of Turkish business life cannot be emphasized enough. Criticism may be seen as hostility. Never say anything negative about a senior to a junior. Don't criticize someone to or in front of their peers. If a manager wishes to correct someone it is normally more effective to do so privately than in public. If an employee has lost face in front of colleagues they may offer their resignation on the spot.

It is extremely rude to interrupt, or to correct, someone when they are talking. Wait politely until they have finished, and then express your point of view. If two people start to talk at the same time they will apologize and insist the other go first.

In negotiations, determine your bottom line figure in advance. Concessions are expected and this allows room for you to compromise. Avoid strict deadlines and threats tactics.

BUSINESS DRESS

Dress in offices is formal, and smart suits are expected. Designer labels are popular. Women often wear trousers. Some Westernized companies allow "office casual" all week, or just on Fridays, but they are likely to require business dress for meetings. If in doubt, dress formally.

If you are meeting at someone's home you may be told to dress casually. This will mean "smart casual"—such as designer label, polo-neck shirt, chinos, and proper shoes—never scruffy T-shirt, non-designer jeans, or sneakers.

CANDOR AND COOPERATION

The importance placed on saving face means that the Turkish concept of honesty may sometimes differ from your own. A person may tell a white lie about their boss to protect their honor—"Ayşe Hanım is busy on the telephone," when in fact she is late for work because of the traffic. Don't make it clear that you realize this, as this would be an affront both to Ayşe Hanım's honor and that of the person you are talking to.

This principle works both ways. Turks are unlikely to let you know if they don't believe you will be able to keep to the timetable you have promised, or if they suspect your claims are exaggerated, for fear of offending your honor. It is important to ask them if they have any questions or doubts, and to make sure they realize you will not be offended by hearing their true thoughts.

Saying "I don't know" is often deemed to be weakness. Turks are likely to give a general answer rather than say that they don't know but will find out. This is particularly true when others are present. If you sense this is happening, save your question for someone more senior, or ask it via a letter or an e-mail, so they will have a chance to research it before replying.

Turks do not like to give bad news. In response to a question concerning the whereabouts of a promised product or report you are likely to get the reply, "It's nearly ready," even if work has only just started. If you walk out of a meeting having been told, "Leave us a sample and we will test it and place an order next month," it may mean just that, or it could mean, "This is too expensive/the wrong color/no good, but we don't want to ruin your day by telling you," and the awaited order will never materialize.

Whenever possible, return favors. Turkish culture encourages reciprocity; if someone has helped you, you should help them when they need it. Using influential contacts is routine in the business world. When choosing business partners or consultants such as lawyers or accountants, it is wise to seek out those with the widest networks.

REGULATIONS

There are three experiences that are inescapable when doing business in Turkey: bureaucracy, regulations, and red tape. Turkey follows the

Swiss civil code: you are not allowed to do something unless it is specifically prescribed in law. The Turkish commercial code lays down detailed rules for all sorts of things, and the plethora of regulations issued by government ministries carry the force of law. It is vital to stay up-to-date and informed because regulations can change frequently.

From setting up a company to obtaining a telephone line, detailed documentation, often countersigned by a notary, is required when making applications to the authorities. Any application is accompanied by a *dilekçe* (literally, "statement of wish"), which often has to be in a set format. *Dilekçe* writers can be seen outside most government offices, often with an old manual typewriter, ready to write a *dilekçe* for those who are not sure of the correct process. There are photocopy shops and photographic shops nearby. Most applications require at least five passport-sized photographs. Carry a good stock of these.

Different officials may require different sets of documents for the same task. Government offices are full of people standing in line for the necessary signatures and stamps. You may have to line up six times for six different signatures at the main postal sorting office just to take delivery of a parcel. Never argue with an official, as the power to sign or not sign is in his hands. Any disagreement may result in your papers going to the bottom of the pile. The Turks have a proverb: "The one who holds the official stamp in his hand has the power of Solomon."

WOMEN IN MANAGEMENT

Women in managerial positions are well accepted. Male visitors should be polite and respectful, avoid excessive eye contact, and shake hands only if the woman offers hers first. Physical contact may not be acceptable if she is strictly religious.

LEADERSHIP AND DECISION MAKING

Traditionally, Turkish companies operated "top down." The old-style Turkish boss is formal, and does little but give orders. Middle management is there to check and put a stamp on paperwork. They may be members of the owner's family, and tend not to get their hands dirty.

Many companies are now changing to modern leadership techniques. Books by Western management gurus sell like hot cakes, and conferences are packed. However, the old style lingers on in public institutions, in some older managers, and in the reactive, accepting behavior of Turkish employees.

To avoid confrontation, Turks will react in the way that causes minimal embarrassment. Employees or colleagues may not give their opinion if they think you may not like it, or if you are senior to them and pointing something out could cause you to lose face. A foreign manager may struggle to get truthful feedback from junior staff. You may ask Miss B. to telephone someone whom she knows to be away, but as you have asked her to do it she will not correct you in public and will make the unnecessary call.

PRESENTATION AND LISTENING STYLES

A workshop or training seminar tends to be a serious and formal affair. In general, Turks tend to think that the longer it takes, the better it is. Formal presentations may be read and are usually impersonal. Generally Turks use fewer jokes or "gimmicks" in a speech than Western speakers, and rarely use examples that show themselves or a colleague in a poor light. Juniors are expected to listen to their seniors and never interrupt.

TEAMWORK AND MANAGEMENT

Go slow! As part of a team, allow time for people to trust you before suggesting change. Take care to listen to everyone and to respect their ideas. Don't ever dismiss an idea in public—if you do, the person who ventured it will never suggest another idea to you again for fear of losing face.

Ultimately, the boss is the boss; the manager has clear authority to make the final decision, and the team will swing in behind him, even if they don't agree with it. People are more concerned with group success and keeping the group together than appearing to be the individual shining star. This has its pros and cons. If a problem occurs, it is difficult to get anyone to take responsibility. If you criticize decisions and don't seem to be taking part, you break the group ethos.

CONTRACTS

While trust is essential when doing business in Turkey, the contract is king. Contracts are based on the Swiss civil code and the Turkish commercial code and are written in Turkish.

Foreign companies can expect to encounter massive bureaucracy. You will need patience, and the services of a Turkish lawyer and accountant as there are many unpredictable decisions made at local government level, and frequent changes in the legal and regulatory environment.

Because personal relationships matter, time and patience are needed even after signature, as it is necessary to keep the other side on board with frequent contact. In the event of a dispute, try to resolve matters through a mediator and avoid going to court, which can be a very drawn-out process. If you should find yourself in court, your contract will be key in determining the verdict.

CORRUPTION

Corruption, both grand and petty, is still a problem in Turkey, although it is decreasing. Piracy is also a major problem. On Transparency International's Corruption Perception Index, in 2012 Turkey ranked 54 on a scale from 100 (very clean) to 0 (highly corrupt). The government's anti-corruption strategy has led to a number of public officials being dismissed.

chapter nine

COMMUNICATING

TURKS AND FOREIGN LANGUAGES

Well-educated Turks will be fluent in English, often speaking it grammatically more correctly than native speakers. Many will have been educated exclusively in English since the age of fourteen. Others may be fluent in German or French, but English is more widespread.

Turks are patient and eager to please; in a group they will make sure they speak your language so that you are not left out. This may extend to nominating a child to act as your translator.

TURKISH PRONUNCIATION

Turkish words are pronounced just as they would be in English, with the following exceptions:

ı said as the "o" in woman

ç said as the "ch" in church

c said as the "j" in jam

ö said as the "eu" in the French *veut*

ş said as the "sh" in wish

ğ said as the "y" in yellow and lengthens the preceding vowel

ü said as the "u" in the French *rue*

Consonants are never run together.

GESTURES AND TABOOS

- Turks say "no" with a simple "tsk" sound, or by raising their eyebrows, or by doing both, or by doing both and throwing their head up. Each is more emphatic than the last!
- A nod of the head means "yes."
- A shake of the head means "I am not sure" (so if you do this a salesman will keep on with his patter to try to help you reach a decision).
- To say "I don't know," shrug your shoulders.
- A shrug of the shoulders with raised hands, palms upward, expresses the feeling, "What can I do about it?"
- To express to the cook or chef that a meal or dish was delicious, put the tip of your thumb to the tips of your fingers (palm up) and bounce your hand up and down.
- To refuse something (such as food) politely, put your palm flat on your chest to indicate "No thank you."
- On the first transaction of the day, a shopkeeper may scrape a coin on his chin; this means "May God bless and multiply this."
- A brush of the hands together indicates the job is finished.
- If Turks don't like someone or something, they shake their collar.
- When giving a warning to children, they wag their index finger and say, "*seni seni . . .*" ("you, you," meaning "naughty thing!")

- Children are summoned with the motion of an outstretched hand with palm down and bending the fingers forward and backward while saying, "*gel gel*" ("come, come".)
- When Turks rub their index fingers together side by side, they mean, "are you girlfriend and boyfriend?"
- When they think someone is exaggerating, they rotate their hand with palm up while saying "oh, oh, oh," meaning that they find it hard to believe what they hear.
- It is rude to show the soles of one's feet and to sit with legs crossed. Also, blowing one's nose in public is offensive. Too firm a handshake is considered impolite.

BODY LANGUAGE
Turks are generally very emotional and tactile. However, don't miss the key point: opposite sexes tend not to touch, but with the same sex Turks are more physical than Westerners. It is considered natural and proper for two men to greet each other with a kiss on each cheek. Also, people of the same sex will walk together linking arms or holding hands. Friendships are carefully fostered and maintained, and physical touch is an expression of respect. People stand and sit closer than many Westerners may find comfortable.

When a man is greeting a woman, a loose handshake is preferred, unless they are relatives or long-standing friends.

SERVICES
Telephone
In the early 1990s, the telephone industry was privatized. The state company, Turk Telekom, merged with Alcatel, and great technological advances were made.

There is wide usage of cell phones, and your Turkish friends will be astonished if you don't have one. Turkey uses the European system, and an American phone will not work in Turkey unless it is multiband. Major cities and most of the rest of the country are well covered by GSM operators. You can buy a *hazır kart* (or prepaid SIM card) to put in your own cell phone for a Turkish telephone number—cheaper than using your international number if you are staying for a long time. It is not necessarily thought rude to have your phone on during a meeting, or even in a restaurant. When traveling on an intercity bus or plane, phones must be turned off.

Pay phones are less common since the mobile revolution; they normally need a prepaid card. In hotels the charges for phone calls are high.

Normally you dial 00 for an international dial tone, before the country code. For a national code to a different city, dial 0 and then the city code. This also applies to calls in Istanbul from one side of the Bosporus to the other.

Mail
Regular mail is not so reliable. Mail letters at the post office rather than in one of the few public mailboxes, as these are not always regularly

emptied. When addressing an envelope, put your details on the top left after the word *Gönderen*, meaning "sender." If you are sending a letter within Turkey, the envelope should be addressed in this order: name, neighborhood, street followed by apartment name and number and door number, and lastly city (indented, capitalized, and underlined). A village address can be looser— terms such as "behind the mosque" may be used.

Mail can be slow or can go astray; to guarantee that a letter reaches its destination send it by registered mail. Private cargo companies can provide twenty-four-hour delivery anywhere in the country, and are more reliable.

Internet
Internet cafés are inexpensive, and widespread in cities. The Internet operates mainly on ADSL; in some areas you can sign up for fiber optic Internet. Restaurants and hotels often have wireless networks.

THE MEDIA
The TV set is a major feature of any Turkish home. In some family homes, and in many shops and restaurants, it is on all the time.

There are four state channels and many private channels offering a variety of programming: news, documentaries, music, entertainment, education, soaps, and movies. Some channels show locally produced programs, including Turkish versions of CNN. Others broadcast foreign programs and films dubbed into Turkish. Some channels make a point of showing foreign films or serials in the original language, with subtitles.

Don't be surprised to see a circle on the screen blacking out a cigarette or a glass of wine in your favourite foreign film or show—it is illegal for television channels in Turkey to show these.

Print

Newspapers are widely read, and cheap. They cover a full range of political opinion and secular and Muslim viewpoints. The *Turkish Daily News* and *Today's Zaman* are national newspapers in English, with editorial policies representing different aspects of the Turkish social spectrum.

CONCLUSION

Turkish society at the grassroots level has changed rapidly in the past few decades, and more change can be expected as Turkey's links with Europe grow stronger. But Turkish people still display the core values of respect for elders and authority, and loyalty to and reliance upon the group—in particular the family—setting great store on personal relationships and the importance of honor and saving face. The Turks are very group- and people-oriented. They are loyal and good friends, hospitable, and sociable. They welcome foreign visitors, and will readily offer help.

Some Turkish traits may strike you as contrary. The Turks drive aggressively and are always in a hurry, yet lack punctuality and often show up late for appointments. They dislike rules and regulations, and yet the red tape in official transactions is unbelievable. Most newcomers will suffer the handicap of not understanding the language and, by viewing Turkey through foreign eyes, may easily make wrong assumptions. Yet this unique and important country offers you the chance to appreciate a different way of looking at the world. In *Culture Smart! Turkey* we hope to have eased your path into a complex, rich, and fascinating society.

Further Reading

Atatürk: The Birth of a Nation. Istanbul: Ministry of Culture of the Republic of Turkey/Revak, 1998.

De Busbecq, Ogier. *Turkish Letters*. Oxford: Oxford University Press, 2001.

Eyuboğlu, Hughette. *From the Steeple to the Minaret: Living Under the Shadow of Two Cultures*. Istanbul: Çitlembik Publishers, 2004.

Finkel, Andrew, *Turkey: What Everyone Needs to Know*. Oxford: OUP, 2012.

Finkel, Caroline, *Osman's Dream: The Story of the Ottoman Empire*. New York: Basic Books, 2006.

Freely, John. *Inside the Seraglio: Private Lives of the Sultans in Istanbul*. London: Penguin, 1999.

Haldon, J.F. *Byzantium in the Seventh Century*. Melbourne: Cambridge University Press, 1990.

Kinross, Patrick. *Atatürk: The Rebirth of a Nation*. London: Phoenix Press, 2003.

Kinzer, Stephen. *Crescent and Star: Turkey Between Two Worlds*. New York: Farrar, Straus and Giroux, 2001.

Lewis, Raphaela. *Everyday Life in Ottoman Turkey*. New York: G.P. Putnam's Sons, 1971/London: B.T. Batsford Ltd, 1971.

Mango, Andrew. *The Turks Today*. London: John Murray, 2004.

Mansel, Philip. *Constantinople: City of the World's Desire 1453–1924*. Melbourne: Cambridge University Press, 1995.

Orga, Irfan. *The Caravan Moves On*. London: Eland Publishers, 2002.

–––. *Portrait of a Turkish Family*. London: Eland Publishers, 1993.

Öktem, Kerem, *Angry Nation: Turkey Since 1989*. London: Zed Books, 2011.

Özdemir, Adil, and Kenneth Frank. *Visible Islam in Modern Turkey* London: Macmillan Press Limited, 2000.

Pope, Hugh and Nicole. *Turkey Unveiled: A History of Modern Turkey*. New York: The Overlook Press, 2004.

Runciman, Steven. *A History of the Crusades*, Vol.1–3. London: Penguin, 1990.

In-Flight Turkish. New York: Living Language, 2001.

culture smart! turkey

Index

culture smart! turkey

Acknowledgments

This book is dedicated to my mother, De Lois, with love.

I would like to thank Marion James for all her input and help in writing this book.